S0-AQC-571

Puppets Help Teach

DIANE WARNER

ACCENT BOOKS
Denver, Colorado

ACCENT BOOKS
A division of Accent Publications
12100 W. Sixth Avenue
P.O. Box 15337
Denver, Colorado 80215

Copyright © 1975 Accent Publications, Inc.
Printed in U.S.A.

All rights reserved. No portion of this book may be
reproduced in any form without the written permission
of the publishers, with the exception of brief excerpts
in magazine reviews.

ISBN 0-916406-13-X

Tenth Printing, 1987

CONTENTS

FOREWORD

Diane Warner is an energetic children's worker who uses puppets to capture the interest of her own pupils. In this book she passes along to you many helpful hints which she has gathered from her experience. She knows the problems and questions that will arise in your mind. She has met them herself, and she has put in these pages for you the most practical puppet helps available anywhere.

The lively plays are written especially for young children and are classroom tested. Any beginner or experienced puppeteer has here a rich source of materials for Bible teaching by means of puppets.

The Editors

HOW PUPPETS CAN HELP YOU TEACH

Puppets can help you teach. Just let your hands tell about Jesus. Are you a young person? Are you thin, or perhaps a little chubby here and there? Are you very shy? Or are you quite an extrovert? No matter what type of person you are, you can become a vessel through which God can communicate to children. If you are shy, the puppet stage becomes a delightful barrier behind which you can hide. If you are very outgoing, you can reach out and express yourself through hand puppets. You are opening up a whole new ministry whereby children will absorb and retain God's messages. Enjoy it.

HAND PUPPETRY

There are many advantages to the particular type of puppet ministry described here, as opposed to more complex methods of puppetry. Marionettes require considerable practice in the operation of the strings. They also require a more elaborate puppet stage. Larger puppets, such as the Sesame Street type, require one person per puppet, plus a larger stage that usually cannot be transported in an average sized vehicle. With this type of puppetry, the stage is small and easily portable; it can be folded into a flat unit that fits into the back seat of a standard sedan. The puppeteer needs very little practice in the operation of the hand puppets. The entire show is performed by only one person, eliminating special practice sessions with other people. If you have your portable stage, your puppets and the script, you are ready—and the children will love it!

THE STAGE

The first thing you will need in this exciting ministry is a stage. Obtain a portable clothes wardrobe. If you live in an area where there is a large moving company, this can easily be purchased. They usually cost around $3.50 used or $7.00 new. I have always bought them used for they are to be covered with wallpaper or contact paper anyway. Make sure, however, that the wardrobe is not dented or crushed. If you live in an area so rural that you aren't near a moving company, a regular cardboard wardrobe can be purchased from a local department

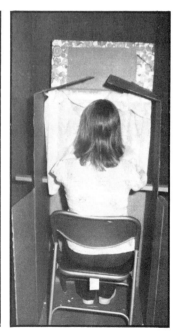

5

store or through sales catalogs for about $10.00. An advantage to this type is that they already have a decorative exterior.

The first step in the conversion from wardrobe to stage is to cut a hole four inches from the top in the front that is 18 inches wide by 8 inches high. Next, cut off the flap that hangs down in back. Then cut the stationary portion of the rear of the wardrobe straight down the middle, creating swinging "doors" by which the puppeteer enters and exits "backstage." (See photos 1, 2, 3.)

Glue bright cheerful wallpaper or contact paper on the entire exterior of the wardrobe, including front, sides, back and top.

Buy a two-by-four (or a one-by-two) board, cut 5 inches longer than the wardrobe is wide. Run this board through the sides of the wardrobe, centered from side to side, 30 inches up from the floor. This board should protrude on each side about 3 inches, thus creating handles for carrying. Most wardrobes already have holes in the proper places for this board, but if not, cut slits on each side through which the board can be placed. When it is in place, it serves as an elbow-rest for the puppeteer and a place for the script. (See photo 3.)

Inside the stage, at the same level as the board, but close to the front stage opening, attach a small cardboard box on each side with brads. These boxes should be about the size of a large matchbox. They are for storing the props the puppets will handle during a performance.

Attach a small rod across the top of the front opening (stage) with large brads. Make simple curtains for each side of the stage which can be drawn across the front of the stage when you wish to. Or, these curtains may be permanently placed by pleating and stapling them on from underneath. (See photo 6.)

Next, your stage will need a backdrop curtain to separate the puppeteer from the puppets and from the audience. Sew a curtain of very thin "see-through" fabric and gather it over the wardrobe bar inside. (This is the regular clothes bar in the top of the moving company's wardrobe. See photo 2. Photo 3 shows the backdrop curtain in place on the bar.)

You may want to use the backdrop curtain as background scene for your plays. Draw simple background scenes on several backdrop curtains and hook them over the bar according to the story you plan to tell. Crayons, water pastels, or liquid embroidery pencils will work well for this purpose. Try distant mountains, or a row of easily scribbled-in fir trees with scattered trees and bushes for outdoor backgrounds, and the broadside exterior of a house with a window showing, or the wall of a room interior with a picture on the wall. Arrange the scene so the puppeteer will be able to see the puppets and also the audience through the fabric.

In order that the audience won't see the face of the puppeteer through this curtain, drop an electric cord with a small light bulb through the top of the wardrobe right over the puppets' performing area of the stage. Place an aluminum pie plate between the light bulb and the top of the stage to prevent fire. When the stage area is well lighted this way, the audience cannot see the face of the puppeteer through the backdrop curtain.

THE PUPPETS

You can work without a stage perhaps, if necessary, but never without your "little people." Enjoy the full measure of your own creativity as you prepare your hand puppets.

I make my puppets in two different ways. The *Bible character* puppets, which are dressed and adapted to various Bible stories in the scripts, are made from the patterns given at the back of the book (see Patterns). Cut the head, hand and body pieces from skin-colored cotton. Try to show natural skin tones of pinkish tan for white people and shades of brown for black and brown people, as well as very light

yellow for people of the yellow races.

Sew the pieces together and stuff the heads with fine foam rubber or kapok. Embroider the faces on, or paint them on with liquid embroidery pencils or a similar painting medium for cloth. Make the hair of either layered yarn, tacked down, or with large twisted loops of embroidery yarn sewn in place.

The hands are mitten-type. Sew the two pieces together for each hand and stuff the hands. Sew the body pieces together, leaving the neck and hand openings open. Attach the head and hands as follows:

Head. Roll a 3x5 inch piece of pliable cardboard around your finger and insert it into the neck opening. Sew head on, taking the needle through the cardboard as you sew.

Hands. Sew the stuffed hands down flat at "wrists," attaching "A" on hands to "A" on the body.

Each puppet will need several changes of clothing. You can adapt the basic coat pattern for this purpose. (See photo 4 for a variety of Bible characters.)

A donkey pattern is given. Sew the two pieces together, leaving an opening in his back. Turn raw seams inside and stuff, finishing the opening with a few stiches by hand.

(Check that you have these materials on hand: skin-tone fabric, various fabrics for clothing, patterns from back of book, pencil for tracing patterns, scissors, needle, thread, yarn for hair, pliable cardboard, kapok or fine foam rubber—or old nylon hose—for stuffing.)

The *contemporary children-type* puppets are made from the same body patterns as the Bible characters, but I use old-fashioned rubber doll-baby heads for these. Look for old baby dolls that have eyes with lids that open and close as you tilt the puppet back and forth. The heads make these puppets, which help me teach, very lifelike to the children.

Take the head off a doll and attach it to a fabric puppet body. The head of the doll has a rim at the neck, so you simply draw a string tightly around the neck from the inside and it holds very well. Stuff the head with cotton only to the point where your middle finger fits comfortably up into it, making manipulation of the head as free as possible.

For boy puppets, select doll heads with as boyish facial features as possible. You may have to give the dolly a "haircut" in some cases.

I use four contemporary children, Butch, Nicky, Sally and Nancy. They help me apply Bible truths to boys and girls. It is interesting how well they help me to communicate with the children in the audience, as you will see in the scripts. (Meet Nancy, Sally, Nicky, and Butch, l to r, in photo 5.)

It is important that the four children puppets each have an individual look. My Nancy and Sally wear colorful dresses or smocks and have bows in their hair. Butch has on typical shirt and jeans, but Nicky requires more of a "messy look," complete with dirt and an ever-present Band-Aid on his cheek. One of your girls might always wear pigtails with big bows. The other girl may be identifiable by her bright red pinafore. The audience looks for these familiar things, and they soon learn the personalities of the puppet children and expect them to act in character. (Photo 6 shows the front of the stage with Nicky and Nancy performing. In photo 7 two Bible characters, John and Peter, talk together.)

THE ART OF MANIPULATING HAND PUPPETS

Hand puppets, as the name implies, are worn on the puppeteer's hand—or hands—and act and speak as life-like as possible. At least they act and speak as lifelike as the manipulator can make them act and speak. Try your first completed puppet on your hand, somewhat like a glove, and see how it begins to take on personality. Experiment with where your fingers feel the most comfortable. Some puppeteers use the middle finger in the head (that is what the cardboard neck on the children puppets is for) and the thumb and little finger spread out into the two arms. Others prefer to insert the forefinger in the head and thumb and middle finger spread into the arms, bringing the other two fingers down to catch hold of the body of the puppet.

When performing with the puppets, it is imperative that you keep the "little people" as active and mobile as possible. The puppeteer, besides reading off the script backstage, must keep the puppets moving constantly. Make them turn, bend, scratch an ear with one hand, and such actions.

The use of props is very important because they give the puppets something to do. Whether the puppet is playing with a yo-yo, drinking hot chocolate or fishing with a little pole, the addition of props really holds audience interest. In one of my puppet shows one of the puppets was having trouble making the yo-yo do a certain trick. One of the children in the audience ran up to the stage, just as serious as he could be, and said, "I'll show him how to do it."

The audience becomes so involved with all the puppets, the Bible characters included, that their retention level of the story is phenomenal. My husband and I have had children who saw a certain Bible story performed by puppets three years earlier show that they still remembered every detail. Butch and Sally and Nancy and Nicky become friends to the audience, and on Sunday mornings the children come running up to ask if "Butch and Sally are here."

The puppets should not only stay active, but should frequently speak directly to the audience, calling certain children by name. I have given opportunities in the scripts for you to fill in names of children in your audience, names of schools in your town, or the name of some adult they know or creek where they fish, etc. Anything that you can do to make the puppets a part of their environment wins their hearts that much faster.

Converting the wardrobe into a stage, making the puppets, and giving the show itself are all very creative and enjoyable. There is, however, a little work and practice

to it, too. The two most difficult problems you will encounter are in making the switch backstage from one puppet to the other on the same hand, and keeping the voices straight as you read the script. Here are some little tricks I have learned.

In making the switch from one puppet to another, I have found it best simply to lay the puppet on your lap, with the opening facing the hand that will slip into it. Meanwhile, while you are switching puppets backstage, there will always be one puppet on stage speaking and holding the attention of the audience. A few times I've had to ad lib with the puppet on stage while I made the switch. But if you are "in character" and enjoying the story, it will be easy to keep that little person out front chattering away. Sometimes I fill in by saying, "I think I hear someone coming. Do I? Do you hear someone? I do. I think they are coming now, etc."

The other problem involves the voices. First of all, it is very important to have certain voices for Butch, Sally, Nancy and Nicky. I've given Sally a loud, tomboyish voice and Nancy a higher, softer, more delicate voice. Butch is in the medium range. Nick is the character with a very brash, loud, gravelly voice. He's the "tough kid." In order to remember these voices as you are actually reading the script, line-over the words in the entire script beforehand with transparent felt-tip pens. Yellow can always represent Butch's voice, for instance; blue for Nancy; red for Sally, etc. In this way, your voice can be trained to change easily from one character to the other, as you change from yellow to red, for example.

Try to feel the part of each character, too. If the character of Martha in the Bible comes across as being nervous, chattery and full of anxiety, the audience will more easily sense the difference between Martha and Mary. Mary is soft-spoken, peaceful and calm. If you can feel these differences yourself as you read the script, it gives the puppets life as they perform.

Use your own imagination as far as improvisation goes. Perhaps you will think of something very entertaining for Sally to say due to a funny incident that happened in your class or to one of the children in the audience. Maybe one of the children has a new pet rabbit, and Butch works that topic into his conversation. Or Butch might want to talk directly with the audience about something topical.

Occasionally at special times of the year, the "Butch & Sally gang" might want to hand candy treats to the audience. In a case like that, one puppet holds the sack or bowl and the other puppet distributes as each audience member comes up to the stage.

If you are musically inclined, another whole dimension is added. The puppets can sing to piano accompaniment, a record, or a capella. You might use them even in teaching new songs.

Scenery is an aspect of puppet theater I've tried using but have eliminated due to the time factor. However, if you have the extra time and creative abilities, you could add a lot to the puppet shows with scenery, particularly to the Bible stories. I've had caves to "hide in" and trees for characters like Zacchaeus to sit in, etc. But I have had wonderful success without using scenery. This is entirely optional.

You will find, as I have, that the puppeteer will also receive a blessing as she or he performs these shows. One puppet script has the Good Shepherd diligently and compassionately searching for His one lost sheep. He finally finds His little lamb and gathers it in His arms. This touched my own heart as I performed the puppet show, for I identified with the lamb and felt the compassion of the Shepherd as He held His lost one in His arms, just as Christ picked me out of a bramble bush years ago and has held me closely ever since.

This book offers you scripts for some favorite Bible stories, and for certain church-related special occasion days and subjects. I want the Lord to use them to draw children to Himself.

As you make your own "little people" and develop their individual personalities, you will soon be writing your own scripts for many other Bible stories and applying their truths with your puppet boys and girls, with whatever names you may give them. God bless you in your new ministry.

Have fun!

CREATION

SCRIPTURE: Genesis 1, 2
CHARACTERS: Mother, Son from Old Testament times
PROPS: None

SON: Mom, tell me a story before I go to bed.

MOTHER: What kind of a story would you like to hear tonight?

SON: Tell me the one about how God made everything—the birds and the sky and the trees.

MOTHER: All right, Son, but remember—this is a *true* story. It isn't make-believe. It really happened.

SON: How do we know it's a true story, Mama?

MOTHER: Because it's in the Bible—in the book of Genesis. Now, are you ready to begin?

SON: I'm ready.

MOTHER: Good. . . . A long time ago the world was much different than it is now. The earth didn't have a shape and it mingled with the vapors around it.

SON: What are vapors?

MOTHER: Well, vapor is like a mist or a fog. There were no trees or flowers, and no living creatures. Everything was dark.

SON: As dark as the inside of my closet at night?

MOTHER: Even darker than that.

SON: Do you mean there wasn't even a sun or moon?

MOTHER: No sun or moon—not even any twinkling stars.

SON: What happened then?

MOTHER: Well, God decided that there should be light, and so He said, "Let there be light" and a beautiful, bright light shone all round about. He called the light Day and the darkness Night.

SON: What was the next thing God created?

MOTHER: On the second Day, God created the "firmament."

SON: Firn . . . nent.

MOTHER: No—firm--a--ment. Do you know what that means?

SON:	No.
MOTHER:	The firmament is the sky. He took the waters that were above. . . .
SON:	. . . the clouds?
MOTHER:	That's right, and He divided the clouds from the waters below, which are the . . .
SON:	. . . Ummmmmm . . . the oceans?
MOTHER:	That's exactly right. Then there were clouds and oceans. And a lovely blue sky above. That was the end of the second day. Can you remember what God made on the third day?
SON:	I know . . . I know . . . the plants and trees.
MOTHER:	Yes, but first God said, "Let the waters below the sky be gathered into one place so that the dry land may appear."
SON:	How did He do that?
MOTHER:	God is very, very powerful, Son, and He simply caused the waters to collect together. Great seas were formed. . . .
SON:	. . . and rivers?
MOTHER:	And rivers, too, and dry land appeared . . . mountains and hills and valleys.
SON:	What did they look like? Were they pretty?
MOTHER:	No, very bare. No grass, or flowers or trees. And so God commanded grass to grow and flowers to bloom.
SON:	And trees?
MOTHER:	Oh, yes, such lovely trees that many were heavy with sweet fruits.
SON:	You mean, like peaches and oranges?
MOTHER:	And plums and apricots, everything that is delicious.
SON:	What else did He make on the third day?
MOTHER:	That was all for the third day, but the next day God made the sun and moon and stars.
SON:	All at once? Boy, He sure is powerful, isn't He, Mama?
MOTHER:	Yes, indeed. That is why we worship Him and praise Him

every morning when we look out the window and see all He has made for us—out of nothing!

SON: When God made the moon, it made the night not so spooky, huh?

MOTHER: Yes, it gave light to rule the night, just as the greater light, the sun, rules the day.

SON: What happened next?

MOTHER: Well, the fifth day was a very wonderful day. The sun and moon and stars had been made, the waters were divided from the land, and on the land were grass and trees and fruit. Now the time had come for God to create animals.

SON: I'm glad He did that!

MOTHER: I'm glad, too, Son! At God's command fishes came in the rivers and birds flew about in the air.

SON: Is that when He made the giant whales in the ocean?

MOTHER: That was the time.

SON: But what about the animals on the land?

MOTHER: That's what He made on the sixth day—He filled the earth with all the large animals, and all the small animals, and the insects and every creeping thing.

SON: The dogs and cats and koala bears?

MOTHER: Yes, all of those.

SON: I'm glad He made all the animals. If He didn't, I wouldn't have my puppy and Dad wouldn't have his cattle and horses.

MOTHER: God was very happy with all He created, but He felt creation still wasn't quite complete. Although everything He had created so far was perfect in every way, there was no creature with a mind to think and reason, and therefore no one to worship the God who was the Creator.

SON: Is that when He made people?

MOTHER: Yes, first He created Adam, the first man, in His own "image and likeness," and He gave Adam power to rule over the living things of the world. Later, He created Eve, the first woman, from one of Adam's ribs, to be by his side as his helper.

SON: Like you help Daddy?

MOTHER:	That's right. And Adam and Eve became the first Father and Mother, and they had a son, just like you are our son.
SON:	Was God finally finished with everything He wanted to create?
MOTHER:	Yes, He was and on the seventh day He rested. That's why we set one day of the week aside to rest, too.
SON:	I love that story, Mama. It makes me love God all the more when I realize how powerful and wonderful He is to create everything. Thank you for telling me the story again. Good night.
MOTHER:	Good night, Son.

NICKY AND SALLY TALK ABOUT CREATION

SCRIPTURE: Genesis 1, 2
CHARACTERS: Nicky, Sally
PROPS: Two yo-yos made out of buttons with string.
These are attached to wrists of Nicky and Sally.

NICKY:	Hey, look, Sally, I can make my yo-yo "sleep"!
SALLY:	You can? Let me see.
NICKY:	[Throws yo-yo down and looks down at it.] See? Can you make yours "sleep"?
SALLY:	No—mine always stops at the bottom.
NICKY:	You have to throw it down hard—like this—and then hold your wrist still.
SALLY:	Like this? [She throws her yo-yo down.]
NICKY:	Sure—there, it's "sleeping" now.

SALLY:	It is! It is! Look at that! I could never make it do it before.
NICKY:	Can you do "Rock the Baby"?
SALLY:	Oh, no, that's way too hard!
NICKY:	Look, I'll show you. *[He throws down the yo-yo and tries to pick up the middle of the string with the other hand, but isn't successful.]* Oh, well, I can't do that one right now. But I can do "Round-the-world" just perfect. Watch! *[Swings yo-yo around in a full circle and hits Sally in the head.]*
SALLY:	Ouch! Nicky, you hit me in the head!
NICKY:	I did? Oh, I'm sorry, Sally. Where did it hit you?
SALLY:	Right *here! [Points to top of her head.]*
NICKY:	Put your head back and maybe it will feel better. *[Sally puts her head back, as if looking up.]*
SALLY:	Hey, Nicky, look up there.
NICKY:	Where? *[He also tilts head and looks up.]*
SALLY:	Don't you see something up there?
NICKY:	Ummmmmmmm, let's see. There are some funny clouds.
SALLY:	Don't you see a cloud that looks very interesting?
NICKY:	There's one that looks like Mr. Hamilton. *[Substitute name of a man the children know.]*
SALLY:	Where?
NICKY:	Right there. See, it looks like he has a big plate of spaghetti in one hand and a lollipop in the other.
SALLY:	Oh, I see him now. He has a real long nose that hangs down on the floor.
NICKY:	That's right. Hey, Sally, look at that cloud. It looks just like Stevie Larksen. *[Substitute name of child in audience.]*
SALLY:	Yes, exactly. And he's riding a pig. *[Laughs.]*
NICKY:	With a long, curly tail.
SALLY:	And there's a girl who looks like Sandy Smith. *[Substitute name.]* She's holding a big umbrella.
NICKY:	And there's a tree growing out of her shoe.

[Silence.]

NICKY: Sally, who ever invented clouds anyway?

SALLY: It's like we learned in Sunday School today. God created everything—even the clouds.

NICKY: What was it He created the first day again?

SALLY: The first day, He said, "Let there be light" and there was light. All He had to do was say it, and it happened.

NICKY: What did He create on the second day?

SALLY: The Heavens. He divided the clouds and mists above from the lakes and oceans below.

NICKY: So, that's when He invented clouds.

SALLY: Right.

NICKY: I remember what He created the third day—dry land and the grass and trees and flowers and plants.

SALLY: He made them out of *nothing*.

NICKY: I can't understand how He did it.

SALLY: Neither can I. He is so smart and so powerful, it makes us look pretty small!

NICKY: What did He create next?

SALLY: Let's see. Next He created the sun and moon and all those twinkling stars.

NICKY: Then the fish and birds.

SALLY: Also, don't forget the butterflies and bees. And on the sixth day, He made all the animals—dogs, cats, horses and the squirrels.

NICKY: Even the panthers?

SALLY: Sure.

NICKY: I love panthers.

SALLY: Finally, when He had everything ready, He created people.

NICKY: I know what God did on the seventh day.

SALLY:	Let's see if any of the kids know what He did. Bonnie *[Substitute name.]*, do you know? Terry, do you? *[Give several children a chance to recall from the previous Bible story.]*
NICKY:	On the seventh day God rested and He said that everything He made was good. I don't see how He could make all those things though.
SALLY:	I know it! It just goes to show that God is really mighty and powerful and the Bible says we should praise Him.
NICKY:	At school we studied all about bats.
SALLY:	Bats? Yuk!
NICKY:	God made them so smart!
SALLY:	He did?
NICKY:	Yeah. God made them so they can fly real fast up to a teeny-weeny hole, in the dark and go right through without even touching.
SALLY:	How do they do it?
NICKY:	All the scientists in the world can't figure it out—they aren't smart enough. God created everything that way. It is really mysterious.
SALLY:	God made a lot of really wonderful things happen when He created all the things He created.
NICKY:	I know it. I don't understand how He did it. But I like the things He made, don't you?
SALLY:	Oh, yes.
NICKY:	How's your head now?
SALLY:	Oh, it's O.K. I forgot all about it.
NICKY:	Let's go see if Butch can do "Rock-the-baby."
SALLY:	O.K. Come on.

[Sally and Nicky exit.]

MOSES STRIKES THE ROCK FOR WATER

SCRIPTURE: Exodus 17:5-7
CHARACTERS: Husband and wife from Old Testament times, Moses
PROPS: None

HUSBAND: Come on, my wife. Maybe we'll find water soon.

WIFE: Oh, I'm so weary and tired of all this. Remember when Moses told us we would leave Egypt for the new land that God promised?

HUSBAND: Yes, I remember.

WIFE: That's been so long ago now, and we've had very little good sweet water.

HUSBAND: Yes. It is so dry and sandy here in the desert. All there are are brown rocks and bushes and desert plants. It's so hot and dusty.

WIFE: What breaks my heart is the way the children cry and beg for water. Just this morning little Amos was crying because he didn't have enough water to drink.

HUSBAND: The situation is getting serious now. At first we had a little water, and then we had even less. But now we have hardly any at all.

WIFE: We've searched and searched in every direction for water. But the more we walk, the hotter and thirstier we get.

HUSBAND: And no water in sight!

WIFE: Remember that one time we saw all those green trees and bushes and grass ahead of us? That means there had to be water.

HUSBAND: We all got so excited, thinking it was sweet water, but it was so bitter we had to spit it out.

WIFE: But then Moses prayed to God and God answered and told him to cut down and throw a tree into the water and it would be sweet.

HUSBAND: And it was. How good it tasted. We could hardly get our fill.

WIFE: Then there was the time we saw the 70 palm trees and 12 wells of good, sparkling water. We set up our tents and stayed for a good long while.

HUSBAND: Yes, but the trouble seems to come when we have to keep moving. Now we are really desperate. What shall we do?

WIFE: Let's go find Moses. He'll know what to do. Come on.
                [They leave.]   [Change "Wife" puppet to "Moses" puppet.]

                [Enter Husband and Moses.]
HUSBAND: Hello, Moses. We're really worried about this water prob-
                lem. What are you going to do? The people are all
                complaining and so unhappy. They think God has let them
                down.

MOSES: I have wonderful news!! A miracle has happened!! I prayed
                to God and asked what we were to do.

HUSBAND: Did He answer you?

MOSES: Yes, He did. He said: "Go ahead of the people. Take the
                leaders with you. Take your rod, too. Strike the rock that I
                will show you. And water will come out."

HUSBAND: What a strange request. Did you do it?

MOSES: I did exactly as He said. I struck the rock with my rod and
                water came flowing out. It is sweet and cold. There is more
                than enough for everyone in this camp.

HUSBAND: What a miracle! I can't wait to tell my wife and son.

MOSES: Water is a good and perfect gift which comes from the
                Father. God has certainly blessed us with this miracle. Let's
                start gathering pots, so we can fill them all with the sweet,
                delicious water.
                [They both exit.]

NICKY AND SALLY TALK ABOUT MOSES AND THE WATER

Bible school 1992

SCRIPTURE: Exodus 17:5-7
CHARACTERS: Sally, Nicky
PROPS: Small container of water, the size of a thimble

19

NICKY:	DUM, DUM, DUM, DUM, DUM—ICK, ICK, PHOOEY!
SALLY:	What is the matter with you, Nicky? What are you doing?
NICKY:	I'm sticking my tongue out at that dumb rain. Look at it. It's getting all over my new bicycle. And look at that—all over my football.
SALLY:	Well, you shouldn't have left your old football out there if you didn't want it to get wet.
NICKY:	I know, but I didn't think it was going to rain. It makes the road so slippery . . . I can't even ride my bike. DUM-DUM-DUM!
SALLY:	You should be ashamed of yourself. Don't you remember the true story in the Bible about the Israelites who didn't have any water out in the desert?
NICKY:	Yeah, I remember that.
SALLY:	Well, just think how happy they would have been to have this nice rain. Imagine how you would appreciate it if you were in the desert.
NICKY:	Oh. . . .
SALLY:	Go ahead . . . look at the rain . . . and start appreciating.
NICKY:	Oh, boy . . . O.K. — Appreciate, appreciate.
SALLY:	You're pretty dumb sometimes, Nicky. Rain is wonderful. It means we have lakes to go boating in, and streams to go fishing in, and plenty of water to drink.
NICKY:	Yeah.
SALLY:	And besides, water is fun to play in if you have on rubber boots. Don't forget that rain is from God, it is really a blessing.
NICKY:	I didn't know rain was from God.
SALLY:	Well it sure is. So don't call it dumb and stuff like that. You'd better appreciate it or maybe God will take it away from us like He did from the Israelites when they didn't appreciate it years ago.
NICKY:	O.K. I guess water really is pretty good stuff, all right.
SALLY:	We should tell everybody not to pollute it either.

NICKY: Not to what?

SALLY: Pollute it.

NICKY: What does that mean?

SALLY: That means not to let old dead fish and papers and garbage and stuff get into the water. Just think how much fun nice clean water is to play in and drink and take a bath in and all that. . . .

NICKY: Take a bath in? Ick! Who likes baths? I know one fun thing I love to do with water.

SALLY: What?

NICKY: I'll be right back and I'll show you.

SALLY: Where are you going?
             [Nicky leaves to get little "bucket" of real water to pour on Sally's head.]

             [Nicky returns.] w/ squirt gun
NICKY: Yes, I have a real fun thing I love to do with water.

SALLY: What?

NICKY: This! [He dumps water on her head and leaves quickly.]
             Points gun & pretends to squirt.

SALLY: [Looking out at audience.]   Now none of you out there would do a thing like that, . . . would you?
             [Sally exits.] Don't you dare, Nicky - (she exits - screaming)

Nicky: Looks at audience - "What are you laughing at" - (& starts squirting at them)

KING DAVID AND
LITTLE PRINCE MEPHIBOSHETH

SCRIPTURE: II Samuel 9
CHARACTERS: King David, Ziba, the servant, little prince Mephibosheth

PROPS: None

DAVID: I made a promise to Jonathan when I was a boy that we would always love each other and be kind to each other's family. Now my dear friend, Jonathan, has been killed in the war, and most of his family is dead, too. I must find out if he has any children living, for I want to be kind to them, as I promised Jonathan.
[Enter Ziba, the servant.]
Hello, Ziba. You used to be a servant in Jonathan's house before the dreadful wars, didn't you?

ZIBA: Yes, sir.

DAVID: Perhaps you can tell me. Is there anyone left of Jonathan's family to whom I may be kind?

ZIBA: Jonathan has a son who is lame in both feet.

DAVID: Where is he now?

ZIBA: Well, sir, he is just nearby staying in a home. Shall I send a messenger for him?

DAVID: Yes, please. Thank you, Ziba.

ZIBA: I'll have Jonathan's son come immediately.
[Exit Ziba.]

[Remove   Ziba   puppet   and   put   on   Little   Prince Mephibosheth.]

DAVID: I'm so anxious to see Jonathan's son. I'm sorry he is crippled. Oh, here he comes now.
[Enter Mephibosheth.]
Mephibosheth!

MEPHIBOSHETH: Behold your servant. *[Bowing.]*

DAVID: You seem afraid of me. Don't be afraid! Your father and I were good friends, and I have called you here to show you kindness because I loved your father.

MEPHIBOSHETH: Thank you, sir. I know my father, Jonathan, loved you greatly.

DAVID: I would like to give you all the land that once belonged to your grandfather, King Saul.

MEPHIBOSHETH: Oh, sir, I am lame, how could I care for so much land?

DAVID: I will arrange for Ziba and his sons to take care of it for you.

MEPHIBOSHETH:	Oh, thank you, kind king! I have no words to tell you how kind you are to me.
DAVID:	And I have something else I want to do for you. I want you to live here with me and I shall take care of you all the rest of your life.
MEPHIBOSHETH:	Oh, King David! You are a mighty king. I am a useless lame boy! There is no king who would want a lame boy around.
DAVID:	Oh, dear son. I don't care that you are lame. Don't you see how much I love you anyway? You are Jonathan's own dear child and I pledged to your father that I would always be kind to his family. You shall be very happy here with me.
MEPHIBOSHETH:	I shall love it here with you!
DAVID:	I shall instruct Ziba that I have given you all the land that belonged to King Saul. Your land will be well taken care of, for he has 15 sons and also other servants who make a good living from fields and vineyards. Ziba loves you, too, and he will do a good job.
MEPHIBOSHETH:	Oh, yes, sir. I know he will do a very good job. He always worked hard for my father.
DAVID:	But you shall live here with me and I shall do everything I can to make you happy. You shall always eat at my table with me, and every evening after our meal, I'll tell you many stories of things your father and I did together when we were your age.
MEPHIBOSHETH:	Oh, I would like that!
DAVID:	I'll even tell you about Goliath—a great giant I killed with my sling shot when I was a young shepherd boy. You shall be like my own son. *[They walk off together. David puts his arm around the boy's shoulder.]*

SALLY AND NANCY LEARN FROM DAVID AND MEPHIBOSHETH

SCRIPTURE: II Samuel 9
CHARACTERS: Sally and Nancy
PROPS: Two bracelets attached to the backs of Sally and Nancy with thread (shiny plastic, if possible, to look like "hula hoops." These are held up by the "hands" of Sally and Nancy).

SALLY: Hi, Nancy.

NANCY: Hi, Sally, do you have your hula hoop?

SALLY: Yes, do you?

NANCY: Um hmmm. I'm sure glad school is out—I couldn't wait to try it out.

SALLY: Is it new?

NANCY: Yes, I just got it on Saturday. I saved my allowance for a whole month.

SALLY: What tricks can you do?

NANCY: Well, I can try to do "ocean waves."
[Nancy makes an effort to get hula hoop to go around her waist. Of course, it won't because it is attached with thread on the back of her dress, but it will appear as if she is trying.]
I can't do it. Can you?

SALLY: It's really hard, but I think I can do Saturn's Rings.

NANCY: Let me see.
[Sally again "tries"—to no avail of course.]

SALLY: This isn't my day.

NANCY: Hey, Sally, look over there. . . .

SALLY: Where?

NANCY: There's that new girl at school.

SALLY: You mean, the one with the crippled leg?

NANCY: Yeah, she's so shy, she just sits around all the time. She never plays or anything.

SALLY: I know.

NANCY: Well, come on, let's practice. I'll give it another try.
             [Nancy "tries" again.]

SALLY: Nancy, you're as bad as I am. *[Laughs.]*

NANCY: *[Laughs.]* I know.

             [Silence.]

SALLY: What's the matter?

NANCY: I just feel guilty standing here, having fun, when that girl is
             standing there watching us.

SALLY: She can't do things like we can, 'cause of her leg.

NANCY: I know. I feel sorry for her. Look at her—doesn't it make
             you want to do something for her?

SALLY: Just like David in the Bible?

NANCY: David?

SALLY: Yes, don't you remember? How he felt sorry for little
             Mephibosheth?

NANCY: Oh, yeah, I remember. Maybe we can do something for her
             too. What is her name?

SALLY: Her name is Anna.

NANCY: Oh, well, what could we do—you know, to show her that
             we care . . . and that we want to play with her?

SALLY: First of all, we have to think of something she could play.

NANCY: How about Tiddly-Winks or Jacks or something?

SALLY: Hey, Jacks is a good idea.

NANCY: You just have to sit down for that.

SALLY: Right. I've got some Jacks at home.

NANCY: Let's go see if she wants to play.

SALLY: O.K.—Come on.
             [Sally and Nancy exit.]

DANIEL IN THE LIONS' DEN

SCRIPTURE: Daniel 6
CHARACTERS: Governor, King Darius, Daniel, man
PROPS: Small piece of paper to be held by Governor and King Darius, Crown for King Darius

GOVERNOR: *[Enters with the paper.]* King Darius, listen to me. All of us presidents, governors and counselors got together and decided that you should make a new law.

KING DARIUS: What kind of a law?

GOVERNOR: Well, one that would make all people stop praying to God. If they want something, they will have to pray to you for it.

KING DARIUS: How long will this law be in effect?

GOVERNOR: For 30 days, and once you have signed the law—it can't be cancelled for any reason.

KING DARIUS: What will be the punishment for anyone disobeying the law?

GOVERNOR: They will be thrown to the lions—to be eaten alive.

KING DARIUS: That sounds fine—I'll sign it—give it to me.
[Governor gives paper to King Darius.]
[King Darius and Governor exit.]

[Change King Darius and Governor puppets to Daniel and Friend puppets.]

[Enter Daniel and Friend.]
FRIEND: Daniel, Daniel, did you hear the news?

DANIEL: No, what?

FRIEND: King Darius signed a new law. It forbids anyone from praying to God for 30 days, or . . .

DANIEL: Or what?

FRIEND: Or they will be thrown to the lions, to be eaten alive.

DANIEL: Well, I'm going to keep right on praying three times a day to God anyway.

FRIEND: You'll be arrested, Daniel, and thrown to the lions.

DANIEL: My God will send an angel to shut the lions' mouths—I won't be harmed.
[Daniel exits.]

	[Enter Governor.]
GOVERNOR:	Hello, there, you're a friend of Daniel's, aren't you?
FRIEND:	Yes, I am.
GOVERNOR:	The soldiers just found him kneeling in prayer and have arrested him.
FRIEND:	They aren't going to . . . ?
GOVERNOR:	Oh, yes, they have taken him to the lions' den—the lions are very hungry, too.
FRIEND:	Oh, no . . . *[Cries.]* *[Exit Friend and Governor.]*
GOVERNOR:	*[Re-enter Friend and Governor.]* Did you hear what happened?
FRIEND:	What?
GOVERNOR:	Daniel was in the lions' den all night, but this morning when the soldiers looked in, he was still alive.
FRIEND:	Had the lions hurt him?
GOVERNOR:	No—they didn't even touch him.
FRIEND:	Then, God did save him after all?
GOVERNOR:	Save him?
FRIEND:	Yes, he said God would send an angel to protect him from the lions.
GOVERNOR:	Oh, no . . . Then his God is real after all.
FRIEND:	Yes—his God is real all right. . . . Praise the Lord. I want to go see Daniel. *[Exits.]*
GOVERNOR:	Wait until King Darius hears this—Daniel's God is real—I'm going to go tell him right away. *[Exits.]*

BUTCH AND NICKY TALK ABOUT
DANIEL IN THE LIONS' DEN

SCRIPTURE: Daniel 6
CHARACTERS: Butch and Nicky
PROPS: Two fishing poles with hooks and worms—make from twigs, string, pins and pieces of rubber worm from a sporting goods store

	[Butch and Nicky enter holding their fishing poles, but with hook and bait out of sight of audience.]
BUTCH:	Hurry up, Nick.
NICKY:	I'm comin'.
BUTCH:	Boy, this water looks good for fishing today. Look at those fish jumping. *[Butch looks over front of stage.]*
NICKY:	SHHHHHH—don't talk so loud—fish can hear, you know.
BUTCH:	*[Whispering.]* Oh, I forgot. Where are you going to cast?
NICKY:	Right here. *[Casts his line out over front of stage, toward audience.]*
BUTCH:	I'll cast right here. *[He also casts out.]*
	[Silence for about 5-6 seconds.] *[Butch looks in the water.]*
NICKY:	Any bites yet?
BUTCH:	No. *[Silence again.]*
NICKY:	Any bites yet?
BUTCH:	No.
NICKY:	You're wiggling your pole too much.
BUTCH:	I am not.
NICKY:	Yes, you are. Hold it still like I am.
	[Silence again.] *[Nicky scratches his head.]*
NICKY:	Butch?
BUTCH:	What?
NICKY:	Have you ever been scared?

BUTCH:	Sure, lots of times.
NICKY:	Like when?
BUTCH:	Once, when we first moved here, I got lost walking home from school one day.
NICKY:	What happened?
BUTCH:	Well, I must have made a wrong turn or something and all of a sudden I realized I was lost.
NICKY:	What grade were you in?
BUTCH:	I was in first grade.
NICKY:	Then what did you do?
BUTCH:	I tried to think what to do, and all of a sudden I started bawling my head off.
NICKY:	Then what happened?
BUTCH:	A mailman came walking down the street and saw me crying and asked me what was wrong.
NICKY:	Did you tell him you were lost?
BUTCH:	Yes. And he took me to the home of a real nice man and lady.
NICKY:	Did they know where you lived?
BUTCH:	No, but they walked with me round and round the neighborhood up and down every street.
NICKY:	Did you finally find your house?
BUTCH:	Yes—all of a sudden—there it was right in front of me. I was so glad to be home.
NICKY:	They must have been real nice people.
BUTCH:	They sure were—but I was scared there for a while. Have you ever been scared?
NICKY:	The scaredest I ever was in my whole life was when I almost drowned.
BUTCH:	Really? When was that?
NICKY:	Two summers ago. We were swimming in the ocean—our whole family.

BUTCH:	Can you swim?
NICKY:	Yes, but I couldn't swim too good then.
BUTCH:	What happened?
NICKY:	Well, I got out too far from the beach and my feet couldn't touch bottom.
BUTCH:	What did you do?
NICKY:	I grabbed hold of a piece of driftwood and hung on tight.
BUTCH:	Was it like a raft?
NICKY:	Oh, no, not nearly that big—it was real small and I kept getting hit with waves coming down on my head.
BUTCH:	Boy, that does sound scary.
NICKY:	After a long time, it seemed like, I finally landed up on shore.
BUTCH:	I'll bet your family was sure happy to see you.
NICKY:	They sure were. You should have seen me—I was all full of seaweed and sand. I sure did get scared when I was out in the water. . . . Hey . . . I got a bite . . . Oh, he swam away.
BUTCH:	Where?
NICKY:	Right there—it was a real big fish, too.
BUTCH:	Maybe he'll come back—just hold your pole steady.
NICKY:	O.K.
BUTCH:	Do you think Daniel was scared when he went into that den of man-eating lions?
NICKY:	I don't know. Do you think he was?
BUTCH:	I sure would be. But the Bible says he believed in God.
NICKY:	He knew God would keep the lions' mouths shut.
BUTCH:	Do you think God can help kids like us, too, if something scary happens to us?
NICKY:	The Bible says God will help us.
BUTCH:	I think we have to pray and really believe He will.

NICKY:	Have "faith"—that's what it's called.
BUTCH:	Well—I think I'll ask Him to help me the next time I get scared.
NICKY:	Me, too. Hey, let's do something else for a while—I'm tired of fishing.
BUTCH:	O.K. Let's go play basketball. Come on.
	[Nicky and Butch exit.]

THE SHEPHERD AND THE LOST SHEEP

SCRIPTURE: Luke 15:1-7
CHARACTERS: shepherd, lamb
PROPS: A furry white lamb cut from cardboard with cotton glued on to him
          Small dry branches
SETTING: Lamb is stuck in the branches at one end of the stage.

SHEPHERD:	Has anybody seen my little lost sheep? Have you? I've counted my sheep three times and there are only 99 sheep. There are 100 sheep, but I can only find 99! I've got to find my little lamb. There is no one else who will look for him but me. If I don't find him, a lion might get him, or a bear might kill him.
	Stevie *[Substitute name of child in audience.]*, have you seen my little lost lamb?
	Toni, have you seen him?
	I'll look over here in the meadow. No, he's not here.
	I'll look over behind these rocks. No, he's not here.
	What was that?
	Baa. *[Faintly in distance.]*

Did you hear something? *[He asks audience.]*

Listen! Baaa, baaa, baaa.

I hear my little sheep. I'm coming. I'm coming. I'll find you!

Baaa, baaa, baaa.

Oh, little one, I'm coming. I'll save you.

He must be here somewhere. *[He gets closer to the lamb.]*

There he is—caught in the briars of that bush. Here little sheep—come on. *[He lifts him up.]* I've got you now. Don't be afraid. Oh, poor little lamb, you're so cold and afraid. Here, I'll hold you close! Oh, you have a little cut on your leg. I'll put healing oil on it. I'll take care of you and never let you get hurt again. Come on, let's go back to the meadow.
[He exits holding sheep in his arms.]

NANCY AND SALLY TELL ABOUT THE LITTLE LOST SHEEP

SCRIPTURE: Luke 15:1-7
CHARACTERS: Sally, Nancy
PROPS: None

NANCY: Hi, Sally.

SALLY: Hi, Nancy. You sure played good at your piano recital last week.

NANCY: Oh, thanks. Did you hear what happened to me that night?

SALLY: No, what?

NANCY:	I invited Jesus into my heart. Now I'm a Christian! I am so happy.
SALLY:	Oh, Nancy, that's wonderful! How did it happen?
NANCY:	Well, it happened like this. . . . I had just finished playing the piano in my recital. I had my new pink dress on—you know the one with the green ribbons?
SALLY:	Oh, yeah, I know the one.
NANCY:	Well, everyone clapped for me and said I did real good and everything, but I just wasn't feeling real happy.
SALLY:	Why?
NANCY:	Well, I heard the story about the Little Lost Sheep in Sunday School last Sunday, and it made me realize that I wasn't a Christian at all—I was just a lost sheep and Jesus, the kind Shepherd, was looking for me.
SALLY:	So, that made you feel sad?
NANCY:	Oh, yes, I felt just awful. Even after my piano recital, I felt terrible.
SALLY:	What happened then?
NANCY:	Well, then we went home and Mom and Dad asked me what was wrong. They thought I was sick or something.
SALLY:	Did you tell them?
NANCY:	Yes, I told them all about it. Mom explained to me how Jesus loves me and how He died on the cross for me. I told her I wanted to pray to ask Jesus in my heart.
SALLY:	So did you?
NANCY:	I sure did—right there in my bedroom, I knelt down by my bed and prayed and invited Jesus into my heart.
SALLY:	You were just like the little lost sheep and Jesus found you and now He's taking care of you. Isn't that wonderful?
NANCY:	I'm so glad that I finally know for sure that I'm a Christian. Well, I have to go practice the piano now.
SALLY:	What time will you get done?
NANCY:	At 4:30.

SALLY: Oh, good, why don't you come over to my house and we'll
                          listen to my Bible story records. . . . Butch is coming too.

NANCY: O.K. I would love to come. See you later.

COMING TO JESUS

SCRIPTURE: Mark 10:13-16; Luke 18:16
CHARACTERS: John, Peter, a mother
PROPS: A baby wrapped in a blanket to be held in arms of mother

JOHN: Look, Peter. Jesus is talking to the Pharisees. Those
                          Pharisees are always trying to trick Jesus into saying
                          something wrong. But they can't do that to God's Son.
                          Jesus has very wise answers for them.

PETER: There are always such important people around
                          Jesus . . . asking Him questions.

JOHN: And He always has the right answers. They can never trick
                          Him.

PETER: I hope no more of those mothers keep coming around.
                          They always want Jesus to talk to their children. But He's
                          too busy talking with important men to bother with
                          children. Just because He healed that woman's daughter, all
                          the other mothers want to hang around. I wish they would
                          understand that Jesus is too busy to spend time with their
                          children.

JOHN: Oh, Oh. Look who's coming. It's one of those mothers
                          again. She's the one who insists on Jesus seeing her children
                          and blessing them. Why can't she understand. We've told
                          her and told her . . . every day. But she just keeps
                          coming back. She's probably coming to ask us again if we
                          can arrange for her children to see and talk with Jesus.

PETER: I'm getting out of here before she gets here. . . .

JOHN:	Well, thanks a lot . . . what am I supposed to say to her?
PETER:	You'll think of something.

[Peter leaves. While John says his next line, switch to Mother puppet.]

JOHN:	Oh, no. Now what am I going to say? Here she comes. Jesus is much too important to spend time with these children. How can I explain it to her. She just won't accept "No" for an answer.

[Enter Mother.]

MOTHER:	John, John, I have to talk to you.
JOHN:	What is it?
MOTHER:	Oh, please, please, won't you help me?
JOHN:	What is it you want?
MOTHER:	You know what I want. I want my children to see Jesus.
JOHN:	Now, you know that is impossible. He is too busy with important men. He has no time for children.
MOTHER:	But, you don't understand. I got up early again today. I washed and pressed the children's best clothes. I washed their hair. They are all clean and nice to see Jesus.
JOHN:	I don't know why you go to all this trouble every day when you know He is too busy to see them.
MOTHER:	*[Crying.]* Oh, please, John. Jesus healed my friend's daughter. He can't feel that way about children. Isn't there some way you can talk to Him? You are His friend. He loves you and knows you. He will listen to you. Won't you try?
JOHN:	This is getting nowhere. Why is it that you are so stubborn?
MOTHER:	I am stubborn because I want my children to be near Jesus. I feel content to be near Jesus. I can feel His love. I want my children to feel His love, too. I want Jesus to bless them and pray for them. We want Jesus to pray that our children will grow up to love and serve God.
JOHN:	I'm sorry. You have gone to all this trouble for nothing. You might as well start back home. It is no use.

MOTHER: *[Starts to cry again.]* Oh, John. I will take them myself and try.

[Mother exits.] [Put on Peter puppet while John says next line.]

JOHN: I feel sorry for these dear mothers who come with their children, but what can we do?

[Enter Peter.]

PETER: John, John, something wonderful has happened!

JOHN: What is it, Peter? You look like you've been running.

PETER: I have been running. I wanted to get back here to find that mother who was here. Where is she?

JOHN: She left.

PETER: Where did she go?

JOHN: Well, I told her it was useless, trying to have her children see Jesus, so she said she was going to try again by herself. She went right down there. *[Points.]*

PETER: We've got to find her. I just found out something important. I went over to where Jesus was talking to the Pharisees and a woman came up with her little boy. I tried to shoo her off. I told her that Jesus couldn't be bothered, you know. And Jesus heard me and He scolded me.

JOHN: He scolded you?

PETER: Yes, He said, Let the children come to Me. Don't tell them to go away. In God's kingdom there will be people who are like little children. And if you don't come to God like a little child will come, you can't even get into God's kingdom.

JOHN: Do you mean that children have a place in His kingdom?

PETER: Yes, and not only that, but He got all the little children who were there and took them up into His arms.

JOHN: He held them?

PETER: He sure did, and then He placed His hands on their heads and He blessed them!

JOHN: Oh, Peter, that is wonderful news. He must really love children to have done that! We must find that mother who was just here to tell her the good news.

36

PETER:	Wait—look—there she is now.
JOHN:	Where, I can't see.
PETER:	Right there. *[Pointing.]* See, Jesus just took her baby out of her arms and He is blessing the baby and holding it.
JOHN:	Oh, yes, I see. She is smiling.
PETER:	She sure is. Come on, let's go down closer where we can see.
JOHN:	O.K. Let's go. *[They both exit.]*

NICKY AND SALLY TALK ABOUT COMING TO JESUS

SCRIPTURE: Luke 18:15-17
CHARACTERS: Nicky and Sally
PROPS: A toothpick boat made with toothpicks in a sloppy fashion.
Holes in the boat are obvious.
Tiny black Bible.
Piece of paper with a picture on it.

NICKY:	Oh, Boy . . . I'm so dumb . . . and stupid . . . and ugly . . . and no one likes me . . . and all I do is dumb things . . . dumb, dumb, dumb, dumb, dumb, dumb, dumb. That's me—D-U-M-B. . . . dumb! *[Loudly.]*
SALLY:	Hi, Nicky.
NICKY:	*[Meekly.]* Oh, hi, Sally.
SALLY:	What on earth were you yelling about? I could hear you all the way from my back yard.

NICKY:	Oh, I don't want to tell you.
SALLY:	Come on . . . we're friends, aren't we?
NICKY:	I guess so.
SALLY:	Didn't I give you a Valentine on Valentine's Day?
NICKY:	Yes, but it was a picture of a dog sticking his tongue out at me.
SALLY:	He was *not* sticking his tongue out.
NICKY:	He was too.
SALLY:	Was not.
NICKY:	*[Irritated.]* Well, what was he doing then?
SALLY:	He was supposed to be . . .
NICKY:	What?
SALLY:	You know . . .
NICKY:	What?
SALLY:	*[Loudly makes a whispering sound in Nicky's ear.]*
NICKY:	What? I can't hear you.
SALLY:	*[Again makes a whispering sound in his ear.]*
NICKY:	I still can't hear you.
SALLY:	*[Again whispers in his ear.]*
NICKY:	Can't you speak up?
SALLY:	*[Loudly.]* KISSING!
NICKY:	Really?
SALLY:	Yes, it was a puppy and . . . oh, well, never mind . . . it doesn't matter anyway. He wasn't sticking his tongue out though. So, doesn't that prove we're friends?
NICKY:	Yeah, I guess so.
SALLY:	Well, then, if we're friends, why not tell me why you were yelling your head off when I walked up?
NICKY:	Oh, I don't know.

SALLY:	Come on.
NICKY:	Well . . . *[Whispers in her ear.]*
SALLY:	Now, I can't hear *you*. Say it louder.
NICKY:	*[Whispers again in her ear.]*
SALLY:	Nicky Smith—if I am your friend, you can tell me . . . OUT LOUD!
NICKY:	Well, O.K. I'm so dumb.
SALLY:	Who told you that?
NICKY:	Nobody.
SALLY:	Then what makes you think such a thing?
NICKY:	Everything I do is dumb. No one likes me. I get in trouble all the time.
SALLY:	First of all, I like you. And second of all, you don't do everything wrong.
	[Nicky reaches to get the toothpick "boat."]
NICKY:	Then what do you call this?
SALLY:	What is it?
NICKY:	What does it look like?
SALLY:	Um . . . a castle?
NICKY:	No.
SALLY:	A fort?
NICKY:	No.
SALLY:	Um . . . a tent?
NICKY:	No, you see, I am really dumb all right. It's supposed to be a boat.
SALLY:	*[A long silence.]* Does it float?
NICKY:	Float? Well, I don't know . . . I never thought about *that!* You see, it is dumb, it won't even float!
SALLY:	I think it's a really nice boat, Nicky. It's not dumb at all.

NICKY:	It's not?
SALLY:	No, of course not.
	[Nicky gets the paper with picture on it.]
NICKY:	Well, what about this dumb picture I made for school?
SALLY:	Let me see it.
NICKY:	You're holding it upside down.
SALLY:	Oh, I'm sorry. *[She turns it over.]*
NICKY:	See, it's supposed to be this way.
SALLY:	Oh, now I see . . . I think . . . what is it?
NICKY:	You see? I can't even draw a picture. *[He points to picture.]* This is a mountain, and these are soldiers and these are Indians and this is the forest.
SALLY:	What's that?
NICKY:	Where?
SALLY:	Those things, right there.
NICKY:	Carrots.
SALLY:	Carrots?
NICKY:	Well, the soldiers were just getting ready to cook some carrots when the Indians came over the mountain.
SALLY:	Right.
NICKY:	Does that look stupid to have carrots in the picture?
SALLY:	No, Nicky, not at all. I like the carrots. I think they are really cute.
NICKY:	You don't think it's an awful picture?
SALLY:	Of course not. Hey, what's that stuff all over your pants?
NICKY:	That?
SALLY:	Yeah.
NICKY:	That's where I fell in the grapes.
SALLY:	Fell in the grapes? Where?

NICKY: Oh, I was in Safeway and Mom said to go get some bananas, and I sort of slipped and fell in a big box of grapes. They squished all over the place!

SALLY: Oh, I see.

NICKY: Now, do you see what I mean, Sally? Wasn't that dumb of me?

SALLY: *[Looks at kids in audience and whispers to them.]*
Do you think that was dumb?
[Then she repeats question to specific children sitting in audience.]
No, of course not, Nicky, no one thinks you're dumb at all.

NICKY: Oh, I don't think anyone really understands what it's like to be like me.

SALLY: I know someone who understands!

NICKY: Who?

SALLY: Jesus . . . He understands all about you.

NICKY: How do you know that?

[Sally gets her Bible.]

SALLY: 'Cuz—look—right here in my Bible. It says that Jesus really understands kids. And He loves them and wants to help them.

NICKY: Yeah? Let me see.

SALLY: See—look here—here's a story, and it's true too, about when all the mothers wanted to bring their children to Jesus, but all the disciples wouldn't let them bring their kids to Him. They thought Jesus only wanted to talk with important people. But do you know what Jesus said?

NICKY: No, what?

SALLY: He told the disciples that He loves children and to bring all the children to Him. He even held the children in His arms.

NICKY: He did? Does He love all kinds of children? Even ones like me?

SALLY: Of course, He does. And He'll help you with all the stuff you try to do. He'll be a Friend to you.

NICKY: Oh, Boy, I want Jesus to be my Friend!

SALLY:	Come on over to my house. I've got a big Bible story book that explains all about it.
NICKY:	O.K. Let's go. Hey, Sally, you really are my friend.

JESUS WASHING FEET

SCRIPTURE: John 13:2-16
CHARACTERS: Peter, John, and Jesus with a towel wrapped around Him
PROPS: Small towel sewed to one hand of Jesus

PETER:	John, did you hear what Jesus said?
JOHN:	Yes. He knows this is His last night on earth before He is crucified and goes back to Heaven.
PETER:	Look over there. . . . What is Jesus doing now?
JOHN:	He's taking off His outer robe.
PETER:	And He's wrapping a towel around Himself.
JOHN:	Now, He's pouring some water into a basin.
PETER:	He has the towel wrapped around Him like a servant.
JOHN:	Well, you know what He has taught us—to be truly great, you must serve others.
PETER:	I know, but it looks like He's going to wash all the disciples' feet!
JOHN:	He shouldn't be doing that.
PETER:	But He is. Look.
JOHN:	I think He's coming over here. He is.
PETER:	Do you think He's going to wash our feet, too?

JOHN: I'm sure He is.

                   [John exits.]   [Change John puppet to Jesus puppet.]

PETER: Jesus is on His way over here with a basin of water and a
                   towel. He shouldn't lower Himself to this. . . .
                   [Enter Jesus]

PETER: Master, you shouldn't be doing this.

JESUS: I know you don't understand now, but some day you will.

PETER: No . . . You won't ever wash my feet!

JESUS: But if I don't, we can't be partners.

PETER: Then wash my hands and my head, too. Don't just wash
                   my feet.
                   [Jesus washes Peter's feet.]

JESUS: Do you understand what I was doing?

PETER: No, Lord.

JESUS: You call me Master and Lord and that is true. But I have
                   been an example to you—since I have washed your feet,
                   you should wash each other's feet.

PETER: I want to follow your example.

JESUS: A servant is not greater than His master. You know
                   this—now do what I have taught you. Follow my example,
                   for this is the path of blessing.
                   [Peter and Jesus exit.]

BUTCH AND SALLY TELL ABOUT JESUS WASHING FEET

SCRIPTURE: John 13:2-16
CHARACTERS: Butch, Sally
PROPS: Small towel, small Band-Aid, ugly rubber monster, stick

SALLY: Hi, Butch.

BUTCH: Hi, Sally.

SALLY: Boy, didn't we have fun last week playing Pretend?

BUTCH: Yeah, except when you bopped me on the head too hard. You play rough.

SALLY: I'm sorry. I didn't mean to hurt you. I was just having fun. Let's play Pretend again, do you want to?

BUTCH: O.K. Let's see. Let's play something where I won't get hurt. I know. You be a sweet little kitty cat and I'll be the boy who is your owner, O.K.? You pretend like you want something and I'll try to figure out what.

SALLY: O.K. Meow, meow.

BUTCH: Oh, little kitty. *[Pet head.]* What do you want? *[Sally meows.]* Some milk? *[Sally shakes head No.]* Well, let's see . . . *[Sally meows loudly.]* . . . some food? *[Meows get even louder.]* . . . Now, calm down, kitty, don't get upset. I'll figure out what the kitty wants. *[Meow gets really loud.]* Hey, be careful, you're just a little kitty. You're not supposed to scratch! *[Sally scratches Butch.]* Now, just tell me what you want.

SALLY: *[Whispers something in Butch's ear.]*

BUTCH: A dead mouse? I don't have a dead mouse.

SALLY: MEOW!!!! *[She lands on Butch's head with a pounce.]*

BUTCH: I give up. I give up.

SALLY: *[Giggles.]*

BUTCH: You're a mean kitty!

SALLY: Now, let's pretend that you fell down on your bicycle and hurt your head and I'm a nurse and I stop to help you.

BUTCH: O.K. I'm riding my bike now. *[Makes motions back and forth.]* Oh, I'm falling—oh, my head.

SALLY: I'm a nurse. I'll help you. Oh, poor thing, you've busted your skin open. Right on your eye too. Here, I'll put some medicine on it and a nice Band-Aid. *[She puts a Band-Aid completely over his eye.]* There, is that better? Now, your eye is all fixed.

[Silence—as Butch looks at audience with only one eye showing.]

BUTCH: Now, that's the silliest thing. How am I supposed to see?

SALLY: Use your other eye.

BUTCH: Well, I feel silly with this stupid thing on.

SALLY: Well, take it off—here I'll help. *[She takes Band-Aid off his eye.]* Now, let's pretend you are a little boy and I am the mother and you do something really naughty and I'll have to spank you.

BUTCH: O.K. What shall I do that is naughty?

SALLY: Oh, anything. Start now. Pretend your name is Davy. "Davy, come here. Where have you been? I've been calling you for supper and you never answered."

BUTCH: I've been out in the cave in our back hill discovering things.

SALLY: That doesn't matter. You should have come. Now I'll have to spank you. Where's my spanking switch? Here it is. Now bend over. *[She spanks Butch with switch.]*

BUTCH: OW! That hurts. Don't! OW!

SALLY: Now, next time be here at supper.

BUTCH: But, Mother, don't you want to see what I discovered in the cave? It's my new pet and I really love it. Wait and I'll get it for you. *[Gets rubber monster.]*

SALLY: Hurry up.

BUTCH: Here it is!!!! *[He puts monster down on Sally's head.]*

SALLY: EEEEK! *[Screams.]* Get it out of here. Butch, that isn't fair. That thing really scared me!

BUTCH: Well, that serves you right for always landing on my head, even when you were pretending you were a kitten.

SALLY: Well, get that thing out of here. It looks real!

BUTCH: O.K. Now, what can we pretend?

SALLY: Let's pretend something serious, like in our Sunday School

45

	class this morning. Remember when Jesus washed His friends' feet? If Jesus came in the room right now, would you want Him to wash YOUR feet?
BUTCH:	Well, in those days, that's what the servant would do for people who had traveled a long way.
SALLY:	I know. But even in THOSE days, would you have wanted Him to wash your feet?
BUTCH:	Jesus told Peter that Peter couldn't be His friend unless Peter let Jesus do it. And I want to be Jesus' friend so I would let Him.
SALLY:	Jesus said, "You must love one another, as I have loved you."
BUTCH:	Just think, someday we'll see Jesus and we'll be able to talk with Him all about it.
SALLY:	We can talk to Him about everything. You know, the Bible says that Jesus really loves children. He always wanted to hold them on His lap and tell them about God.
BUTCH:	Let's not play pretend anymore. Let's learn our memory verse: "Love one another, as I have loved you."
SALLY:	That's really a good verse, isn't it? I hope I can remember it. Come on, Butch, let's say it over and over while we walk over to your house.
BUTCH:	O.K. [Both exit.]

JESUS WITH MARY AND MARTHA

SCRIPTURE: Luke 10:38-42
CHARACTERS: Mary, Martha, Jesus
PROPS: Small wooden spoon (can be made from cardboard)

Attach to Martha's hand with tape or thread.

MARTHA: *[Martha is on stage alone.]*
[She rushes back and forth, waving the spoon, and is loud and hysterical now and during most of the program.]
I'm so busy, busy, busy! I have so much to do to get this dinner ready for Jesus. . . . Whew! It's so hot in here! Just look at Mary in there, sitting at Jesus' feet. She's so lazy! She won't come help me—she just sits there listening! *[Loudly.]* Mary, Mary, come in here!

MARY: *[Enter Mary.]*
[In a soft-spoken voice she uses throughout the program.]
What is it, Martha?

MARTHA: Mary, can't you see how hard I'm having to work? I'm working my fingers to the bone in here, while all you do is sit in the living room visiting with Jesus.

MARY: I'm sorry, Martha, it's just that—

MARTHA: *[Interrupts.]* I have to rinse all those grapes and fix the fruit tray. And look here *[Rushing around with her spoon.]*, the mutton's boiling over!

MARY: It doesn't matter. . . .

MARTHA: *[Interrupting.]* Doesn't matter! What do you mean, it doesn't matter? Why, we have to get the table set, and look at this mess where the mutton boiled over. Oh, it's so hot in here!

MARY: Martha, Martha, try to calm down. The important thing is that Jesus is here with us, right now, in our very own living room!

MARTHA: This bread will NEVER get done. Any other day and it would already be done. But oh, no, today it cooks and cooks, and never gets done!

MARY: Why don't we forget all this fussing and spend time with Him while we can? He won't be with us forever.

MARTHA: Oh, go ahead if you must, I've got to get this fruit plate looking like something.

[Mary exits.] *[Replace Mary puppet with Jesus puppet.]*

MARTHA: Now, let's see. I'll use our best dishes, and those pretty cloth napkins—my, but it's hot in here! Now, where did I put those pink napkins anyway?

[Enter Jesus.]

47

MARTHA:	Oh, Hello, Jesus.
JESUS:	Martha, my dear, precious friend. You are way too upset over all the little details of supper.
MARTHA:	But, Jesus, doesn't it seem unfair that Mary just sits and talks with You while I do all the work? Tell her to come help me!
JESUS:	Dear Martha, you have your values twisted. There is really only one thing worthy of so much concern. Mary has discovered it and I won't take it away from her.
	[Jesus exits.]
MARTHA:	*[To audience.]* What do you think He meant by that? Do you think He means that it is more important to give time to Jesus than to fuss over all the details of life? I wonder. . . . *[Martha exits.]*

NICKY AND NANCY TALK ABOUT MARY AND MARTHA

SCRIPTURE: Luke 10:38-42
CHARACTERS: Nicky, Nancy
PROPS: Small Sunday School papers for Nicky to hold
Small candy sticks to fit in Nancy's pocket

NICKY:	Hi, Nancy, whatcha' got in your pocket?
NANCY:	Some candy sticks.
NICKY:	What are you going to do with them?
NANCY:	Eat them.
NICKY:	All of them?

NANCY:	Maybe.
NICKY:	Oh.
	[Silence.]
NANCY:	Do you want one?
NICKY:	*[Excitedly and loudly.]* Oh, yes, can I have one?
NANCY:	Go ahead and pick one!
NICKY:	Oh, boy. Let's see, shall I take this one? . . . No, this one. . . . No, this one. . . . I know, I'll take this one.
NANCY:	O.K. Now, are you happy?
NICKY:	Yeah. Thanks, Nancy.
NANCY:	What did you think about the story today?
NICKY:	About Mary and Martha?
NANCY:	Yeah.
NICKY:	Oh, let me see.
NANCY:	What did you learn?
NICKY:	That I don't have to help Mom set the table anymore?
NANCY:	*[Laughs.]* No, Dummy! The point was that it is more important to spend time with Jesus than to worry about all little stuff that's happening.
NICKY:	How can I spend time with Jesus if I can't see Him?
NANCY:	Well, just because you can't see Him doesn't mean He isn't with you, and besides there IS a way you can spend time at His feet listening to Him, just like Mary did.
NICKY:	How, Nancy? I can't think of a way.
NANCY:	Of course, there's a way. The answer is simple. Do any of you know the answer? *[She asks the audience and lets various children respond.]*
NICKY:	Oh, I know—read the Bible and pray!
NANCY:	That's right! We can do that easy every day, and then some day when we get to Heaven, we can sit at His feet, in person.

NICKY:	That's a good idea—I'm going to be sure to spend time with Jesus every day.
NANCY:	I want to be like Mary and do what really counts.
NICKY:	You mean like taking around these dumb Sunday School papers?
NANCY:	They aren't dumb. Let me see one of those papers. "You are invited to Sunday School next Sunday morning. We are having a puppet show. It is at 9:15 A.M." What are you supposed to do with them?
NICKY:	I promised my Sunday School teacher I would give these to some of my friends to see if they would like to come with me to Sunday School. I was supposed to do it this afternoon.
NANCY:	What do you mean "supposed" to?
NICKY:	Well, I don't want to do it. My friend, Billy, and I want to go skating down at the lake this afternoon. And anyway, why should I take those papers to all the kids on my block? They probably don't want to come anyway.
NANCY:	Nicky! I'm surprised at you! If you promised your teacher you would do it, you have to do it. Why did you tell him you would do it anyway?
NICKY:	Well, we were learning the verse from the Bible that says: "Teach me to do Thy will," from Psalm 143:10.
NANCY:	So, you are trying to do God's will, right?
NICKY:	Right.
NANCY:	And it's God's will for you to tell others about Sunday School, isn't it?
NICKY:	Yeah.
NANCY:	Well, if you really mean it, you'd better go ahead and take those papers around to all your friends.
NICKY:	I guess you're right. Maybe I can get Billy to help me.
NANCY:	I'll help you, too.
NICKY:	You will?
NANCY:	Sure, I want to do what that verse says, too. I want to do God's will, just like you.

NICKY:	Oh, thanks, Nancy. Let's get started right away. Do you want to go skating with Billy and me when we get finished?
NANCY:	Sure I do. Thanks, Nicky. Let's go.

PETER'S LIES ARE FORGIVEN

SCRIPTURE: Mark 14:66-72
CHARACTERS: Jesus, Peter, young woman, man, slave, disciple
PROPS: None

JESUS:	Peter, this very night all of you, my disciples, will run off and leave me alone, because the Scripture says, "God will kill the shepherd and the sheep of the flock will be scattered." But after I am raised to life, I'll go to Galilee ahead of you.
PETER:	Oh, Jesus, don't worry about me. I'll never leave You, even if all the rest do.
JESUS:	Remember this that I'm saying to you right now. Before the rooster crows tonight, you'll tell three different people that you don't even *know* me.
PETER:	I will never do such a thing, Jesus. I'll never say that I don't know You even if I have to die with You.
	[Jesus exits.] [Change from Jesus puppet to Young Woman puppet.]
PETER:	It's chilly—I think I'll go over by this fire and warm up.
	[Peter rubs his hands together as Young Woman enters.]
YOUNG WOMAN:	Hello.
PETER:	Oh, hello.

51

YOUNG WOMAN: Aren't you one of the disciples of Jesus?

PETER: You must be mistaken. I certainly am not. Come on . . . let's warm up by this fire.

YOUNG WOMAN: You go ahead. I'm going home now.

[Young Woman exits.] [Change from Young Woman puppet to Man puppet.]

[Enter Man puppet.]

MAN: Well, hello there, Peter. What are you up to this evening?

PETER: Just warming up my hands.

MAN: Say, aren't you one of the followers of Jesus? I saw you with Him just yesterday.

PETER: Oh, no. I'm not His disciple. It must have been someone else.

MAN: But you even talk like those from His part of the country.

PETER: No, it couldn't have been me.

MAN: You must be right. I've got to be going now. So long.

[Man exits.] [Change from Man puppet to Slave puppet.]

[Enter Slave.]

SLAVE: *[Pointing to Peter, while talking confidentially to audience.]* He's the one. He's the friend of Jesus. He's with Him all the time. My High Priest has seen them together, too. Peter, isn't that true? Aren't you Jesus' friend?

PETER: NO! *[Emphatically.]*

[ROOSTER CROWS LOUDLY IN BACKGROUND.]

[Slave exits.] [Change from Slave puppet to Disciple puppet.]

PETER: *[Sobbing.]* What Jesus said would happen has come true. I *did* deny Him three times before the rooster crowed. He is the Son of God and I have betrayed Him! How can He ever forgive me? Oh, I'm so sorry I was ashamed to admit He is my Friend. I love Him so much!

[Enter Disciple.]

DISCIPLE: Peter, Peter, I have good news! Jesus said He knows your heart. He knows how sorry you are for what you've done and He forgives you!

PETER: Oh, thank you, for telling me! Come, let's find Him so I can tell Him how much I really love Him.

[Peter and Disciple exit.]

NICKY AND NANCY TELL ABOUT WHEN A CHILD STEALS

Bible School 1992

SCRIPTURE: I John 1:9
CHARACTERS: Nancy, Nicky, Butch and Judge (played by someone in the audience)
PROPS: A first place ribbon

NANCY: Now, listen Nicky Brown, you've got to really get serious about that talent contest! You've got to practice it again right now—and really good, too!

NICKY: I'm afraid I'll mess it up—just like I always do.

NANCY: No, you won't! You'll do it real good—now come on, let's practice that last part again.

NICKY: O.K. *[Sings.]*   "I'll sing a song about a pig,
Who was never very sad,
Because he was so happy,
Over all the friends he had."

NANCY: Now, see, that was just perfect.

NICKY: It was not! I think it's a dumb song anyway, it doesn't make any sense.

NANCY: Well, I'm your manager, Nicky Brown, and if I say it was perfect—IT WAS PERFECT!

53

NICKY:	I'll do it—but I think it's stupid.
NANCY:	Now, get ready. You're next on stage. *[Pause.]* O.K. It's your turn. Go out there and sing.
NICKY:	I'm scared.
NANCY:	Don't be scared, Nicky. The audience looks friendly. They won't bite.
NICKY:	They might.
NANCY:	Whoever heard of an audience like that!
NICKY:	Look at that girl over there—the one wearing the red dress. *[Points to and describes a child in audience.]*
NANCY:	Which one?
NICKY:	That one. *[Points again.]*
NANCY:	Oh, she doesn't look *that* mean!
NICKY:	Do you think she'll hit me if I goof it up?
NANCY:	Of course not! You're letting your imagination run away with you.
NICKY:	Well, O.K.
NANCY:	Now, go out there and sing your song.
NICKY:	O.K. "I'll song a sing about a sig, / Who was never very mad / Because he was so flappy, / Over all the hens he had." *[Runs back to Nancy.]* Oh, no, I goofed it!
NANCY:	Go back out and try to do it again.
NICKY:	*[Goes back to center-stage.]* "I'll sig a sag about a ping, / Who never had a dab, / Because he was so pappy, / Over all the chickens in the sink." Oh . . . *[Runs back to Nancy.]* Now, I've really goofed it up! Listen to the audience—they're just laughing at me.
NANCY:	SHHHH . . . the judge is going to announce the winner.
JUDGE:	*[Played by someone in the audience.]* The winner is Nicky

	Brown because he made us all laugh! *[Hands Nicky the blue ribbon.]*
NANCY:	Nicky, you won! You won!
NICKY:	Oh, boy! I'm so happy. I'm going to go home and tell everybody. *[Behind scenes, change from Nicky puppet to Butch puppet.]* *[Butch enters.]*
NANCY:	Hi, Butch. Did you hear the good news about Nicky winning the talent contest?
BUTCH:	Yeah. *[Dejected.]*
NANCY:	Aren't you happy for him?
BUTCH:	Yeah.
NANCY:	What's the matter? Do you feel bad 'cause you didn't win it?
BUTCH:	No.
NANCY:	Well, what's the matter then? I can tell something's the matter all right.
BUTCH:	*[Starts to cry.]*
NANCY:	*[Comes over and puts arm around Butch.]* Come on, tell me, Butch. Maybe I can help.
BUTCH:	No, you can't help.
NANCY:	Well, how do you know if you don't tell me?
BUTCH:	I've done something really bad.
NANCY:	You have? Did you put a frog in Miss Smith's shoe again?
BUTCH:	No.
NANCY:	Did you put peanut butter and jelly on your sister's toothbrush again?
BUTCH:	No, nothing like that.
NANCY:	Oh, I know—I'll bet you broke something real good and you're afraid to tell your Mother.
BUTCH:	Much worse than that.

55

NANCY:	Oh, Butch, it sounds awful! Tell me what happened.
BUTCH:	[Tearfully.] Well, I was at school, and this kid, his name is Jeff, dropped his wallet, and I saw him, only he didn't see me.
NANCY:	So, what did you do?
BUTCH:	I picked it up.
NANCY:	Did you give it back to him?
BUTCH:	No. . . .
NANCY:	OHHHHHH, Butch. . . .
BUTCH:	Yeah.
NANCY:	You kept it?
BUTCH:	Yeah.
NANCY:	You're in trouble!
BUTCH:	I know, and the baddest part of all is that I feel so awful about it.
NANCY:	You mean, guilty?
BUTCH:	Yeah, ever since I invited Jesus into my heart, I feel extra bad if I do something wrong.
NANCY:	Didn't you know that Jesus will forgive you if you ask Him?
BUTCH:	He will?
NANCY:	Sure, He will, if you really are sorry—deep down in your heart!
BUTCH:	Oh, I really am sorry—really, really.
NANCY:	Well, first of all you've got to go over to Jeff's house and give him his wallet back.
BUTCH:	O.K. . . . O.K. I'll go right now. I'm going to feel so much better when I do that.
NANCY:	And be sure to pray and ask God to forgive you. Then you'll feel better all over! Just like Jesus forgave Peter for what he did—He'll forgive us, too!

BUTCH: Oh, boy, thanks, Nancy. I'm going over to Jeff's house
                      right now. Bye.

DONKEYS, PALMS, AND PARADES
(PALM SUNDAY)

SCRIPTURE: Matthew 21:1-17
CHARACTERS: Jesus, Disciple 1, Disciple 2, Donkey
PROPS: None

DISCIPLE 1:   Here comes Jesus. I think He has something for me to do.

JESUS: Go into the village and you will find a donkey tied and a
                      colt with her; loose them and bring them to me. And if
                      any man asks anything about it, just say, "The Lord needs
                      them," and there will be no problems.

DISCIPLE 1:   Yes, Jesus, I'll go get them right away.
                      [Jesus exits.]

                      [Change from Jesus puppet to Disciple 2 puppet.]
                      [Directed to audience.] This will fulfill the prophecy that
                      said that "Your King will come to you, humble and meek,
                      and sitting on a donkey and a colt will be with the
                      donkey."

                      [Enter Disciple 2.]

DISCIPLE 1:   Did you hear what Jesus said to do?

DISCIPLE 2:   No, what?

DISCIPLE 1:   He said to go to the village and we'll find a donkey tied
                      and her baby with her. We're supposed to untie them and
                      bring them to Jesus.

DISCIPLE 2:   What will the owner say? He certainly won't let us just
                      walk off with his animals. They're worth money, you

know. He might think we're stealing them.

DISCIPLE 1: No, Jesus said that if anyone asks us why we want them, just to say that "The Lord needs them" and then they will let us take them.

DISCIPLE 2: Let's go. Keep your eyes open for a mother donkey and her baby.

DISCIPLE 1: O.K. Hey, look over there. There they are.

DISCIPLE 2: Where?

DISCIPLE 1: Right over there! *[Points.]*

DISCIPLE 2: Let's go untie them.

DISCIPLE 1: Remember, if the owner asks you what we're doing, just say, "The Lord needs them."

DISCIPLE 2: I'll go get Jesus. Get the donkey ready. I'll be right back. *[Exit Disciple 2.]*

[Change from Disciple 2 puppet to Jesus puppet.]

[Disciple 1 leads donkey by holding his neck with both hands.]

DISCIPLE 1: Here, nice donkey. Come on. Nice donkey. Jesus sent us to get you. You're going to give Him a ride into Jerusalem today.

[Enter Jesus.]

DISCIPLE 1: Jesus, here is the donkey.

[Place Jesus on donkey's back by holding donkey puppet with Jesus puppet. It will look exactly like He's riding it.]

DISCIPLE 1: Look, Jesus, all the people are laying their clothes all over the road ahead of You. The crowds are coming from everywhere to praise You. They are covering the road with palm branches, and they are waving them in the air, singing "Hosanna! Blessed is He that comes in the name of the Lord!"

[Disciple 1 and Jesus exit.]

BUTCH AND SALLY TALK ABOUT DONKEYS, PALMS, AND PARADES

SCRIPTURE: Matthew 21: 1-17
CHARACTERS: Sally, Butch
PROPS: Green construction palm branches small enough for Sally to carry

[Sally is carrying armful of palm branches.]

SALLY:	Hi, Butch. That sure was fun yesterday.
BUTCH:	Yeah, I love to go frog hunting.
SALLY:	What did you do with all the frogs you caught?
BUTCH:	Oh, I put them in a can with some water and a rock.
SALLY:	Oh.
BUTCH:	Except for one.
SALLY:	What did you do with that one?
BUTCH:	I put him in the bathtub with my little sister.
SALLY:	BUTCH! *[Teasingly.]*
BUTCH:	She started screaming her head off and got me in a lot of trouble.
SALLY:	I let mine go cause they croaked so loud all night, I could hardly sleep.
BUTCH:	Did you take them back down to the creek?
SALLY:	Yeah. They were lonesome for their brothers and sisters.
BUTCH:	Oh, Sally, that's silly. Frogs don't get lonesome. Whatcha' doin' with those weeds?
SALLY:	These aren't weeds. They're palm branches.
BUTCH:	What are they for?
SALLY:	They're for the front of the church—because today is Palm Sunday. Do you think all those kids sitting out there watching us know what Palm Sunday is?
BUTCH:	I don't know—I'll ask them. Is there anyone out there who can tell what Palm Sunday is? *[Ask individual children in the audience by their first names.]*

SALLY: Does anyone out there know why we have palm branches like this today?
             [Get some answers from the audience.]

SALLY: On the first Palm Sunday Jesus told His disciples to go get a certain mother donkey and her baby.

BUTCH: Did they do it?

SALLY: Sure, they did. They couldn't understand why, but they did it anyway.

BUTCH: Weren't they afraid the owner wouldn't let them take the animals?

SALLY: No, because Jesus told them that if anyone asked what they were doing, just to tell them He needed the donkey.

BUTCH: And then the owner would let them take his animals?

SALLY: Yes. And that's exactly what happened. And then Jesus came into Jerusalem on the donkey and everyone waved palm branches because they wanted Him to be their King. And they sang songs to Him and praised Him.

BUTCH: Then the very next week those same people turned against Him and Jesus died on the cross for us. And then the next Sunday after that, Jesus rose from the dead.

SALLY: That's Easter Sunday, which is next Sunday. So, first comes Palm Sunday, which is today. Then during the week Jesus died on the cross. Then Easter Sunday, which is next Sunday He rose from the dead.

BUTCH: And He's alive right now.

SALLY: Let's sing to Jesus right now. We can sing to Him just like they did that first Palm Sunday.

BUTCH: What is a song we can sing to Him?

SALLY: Ummmmm . . . let's see . . . how about "Praise Him, Praise Him, All Ye Little Children"?

BUTCH: How does it go?

SALLY: *[Singing.]*   "Praise Him, praise Him,
                                    All ye little children,
                                    God is love, God is love."
                                    [Repeat.]

             [Substitute any song of praise that you and the children

know, or add additional songs. Have all the children in the
audience sing with Sally and Butch.]

BUTCH:

This is sure a special day, all right! Do you want me to help you put these palm branches up in front of the church?

SALLY:

O.K. Here, carry some of them.

[She transfers from her arms to his a portion of the palm branches.]

(Let the children distribute the palm branches—regular size—on bulletin boards, or among the other children. You may take a few minutes for them to explain the meaning of Palm Sunday.)

BUTCH AND SALLY TALK ABOUT THE MEANING OF EASTER

SCRIPTURE: John 20; Acts 1:1-11
CHARACTERS: Butch, Sally
PROPS: Two decorated Easter eggs with imaginary holes that Sally and Butch look into

SALLY:

Hi, Butch.

BUTCH:

Oh, hi, Sally. Look what I've got!

SALLY:

Let me see.

BUTCH:

It's an Easter egg, only *look!*

SALLY:

What?

BUTCH:

See. Look right through here.

SALLY:

Oh, I see. Let go, let go so I can see really good.

[Silence as Sally looks into egg.]

BUTCH: Do you see it? Do you see it?

SALLY: Oh, yes. Isn't it beautiful? Where did you get this?

BUTCH: Oh, it was in my Easter basket this morning. Isn't it wonderful?

SALLY: It's the most beautiful Easter egg I've ever seen. The inside is so cute, with that little town and everything.

BUTCH: What did you get in your Easter basket?

SALLY: I got a little pink bunny and candy and . . . *[She gets her egg from prop shelf.]* . . . look . . . I got a special Easter egg, too!

BUTCH: You did? Let me see it. *[He holds the egg to his eye.]*

SALLY: See. Only mine has flowers inside instead of a little town.

BUTCH: Oh, yeah, that's nice. What kind of flowers are they?
           [As he peers into the egg.]

SALLY: All kinds—daffodils, tulips, lilies and stuff. I sure had a nice Easter.

BUTCH: Yeah, me, too.

SALLY: You know what I love about Easter eggs?

BUTCH: What?

SALLY: Well, do you know why they ever first had Easter eggs on Easter years ago?

BUTCH: Why?

SALLY: Because the egg is a way of showing the new life we have because of Jesus.

BUTCH: You mean like when an egg has a little chicken inside and then the chicken hatches out?

SALLY: Yes. The little chicken comes out of the egg and has new life, just like we have new life when we invite Jesus into our hearts. I just love Easter Sunday. It's the most wonderful day of the year.

BUTCH: Do you like it even better than Christmas?

SALLY:	I like Christmastime too, because that was when Jesus was born, but Easter is special because that is when Jesus rose from the grave—after He died for us on the cross, you know.
BUTCH:	I know—if it weren't for Easter, we would never get to be with Jesus in Heaven.
SALLY:	Just think how excited everyone was when they saw Jesus for the first time after He came up from the grave!
BUTCH:	Some of the people couldn't believe their eyes.
SALLY:	Like Thomas—He said he had to feel the hands and side of Jesus before he would believe it, and Jesus told him to touch His hands and side, and Thomas really believed it for sure.
BUTCH:	Will we ever get to see the places in Jesus' hands where the nails went through?
SALLY:	Sure we will—when Jesus comes for us.
BUTCH:	I will feel sad when I see where they hurt Jesus. Just think—He died on the cross for you and me, so He could be our Saviour. Isn't Jesus wonderful?
SALLY:	Yes, and I can hardly wait to be with Him in Heaven. Do you know what happened after Jesus rose from the grave?
BUTCH:	What do you mean?
SALLY:	Well, I mean about how He went back up to Heaven?
BUTCH:	No, how? *[He turns to the audience and calls various children by name.]* Jim, do you know what happened? No? Sarah, do you know? Tell us. *[Allow time for several children to tell their ideas of how Jesus went back to the Father.]*
SALLY:	Sarah knows what happened! A cloud came down from Heaven and took Jesus up into the sky to be with God, the Father.
BUTCH:	Is that where He is right now?
SALLY:	Yes, and soon He is coming for us—just like He left—just the same way—in a cloud!
BUTCH:	You mean we will see Him come in a cloud?
SALLY:	Right! And all of us who are Christians will be taken right up to be with Him. Isn't that exciting?

BUTCH:	When will this happen?
SALLY:	It could happen today, or tomorrow or anytime. We should be ready because we don't know when.
BUTCH:	Just think—if it weren't for Easter, we would never get to go be with Jesus! What will happen to all the people who aren't Christians when Jesus comes back in a cloud?
SALLY:	They won't be able to go with Him.
BUTCH:	You mean they will have to stay here? They won't be able to go with us?
SALLY:	That's what the Bible says. That's why we should tell lots of kids about Jesus and what Easter means.
BUTCH:	Good! Let's go start telling everybody. There couldn't be a better day to get started than Easter.
SALLY:	Wait for me!

NICKY AND NANCY AT VACATION BIBLE SCHOOL CLOSING PROGRAM

used V.B.S. 1993

SCRIPTURE: Romans 10:13
CHARACTERS: Nicky and Nancy
        Nicky must have Band-Aid on face. His hair is rumpled.
PROPS: A sample of several pieces of handwork made at Vacation Bible School
SPECIAL INSTRUCTIONS: At every asterisk (*) substitute a handcraft, song, or memory verse actually used in your Vacation Bible School.

NANCY:	Hi, Nicky—did you have fun at Vacation Bible School this week?

NICKY:	Yeah, I did.
NANCY:	I had such a *marvelous* time! *[Nancy speaks in an aloof manner.]* I really enjoyed the songs, didn't you?
NICKY:	Well, I don't sing too good.
NANCY:	My grandmother says I have *such* an ear for music. And, of course, my voice is so melodic! I'll sing you one of the songs I learned this week.
NICKY:	No, that's all right.
	[Nancy begins to sing a song the children learned that week.]
NANCY:	*[She sings the *song.]*
NICKY:	That was nice, Nancy.
NANCY:	Well, of course it was. I'm good at handcrafts, too! See all the beautiful things I made. Here's *the picture of Jesus I made for my room and the potholders I knitted all by myself. My teacher didn't even have to help me. And look at this ceramic vase I made. My teacher said it was the best in the whole class. Did you make things, too?
NICKY:	Well, I tried, but I'm not so good making things with my hands.
NANCY:	Oh, that's too bad. I'm just lucky that way, I guess. My aunt is an artist and she says I take after her in everything I try. It's my hands! My fingers are so long and slender. That's too bad that you didn't make anything nice!
NICKY:	Yeah . . . it's too bad.
NANCY:	How about your memory verses? I learned my memory verses every day—just *perfectly!* Would you like to hear them?
NICKY:	Well, no. . . . *[She proceeds to recite.]*
NANCY:	Well, the first day's verse was *"For whosoever shall call upon the name of the Lord shall be saved" (Romans 10:13). Now, you say it.
NICKY:	Well, uh . . .
NANCY:	Go ahead, don't be shy.
NICKY:	I don't know it.

NANCY:	You don't *know* it? Didn't you even learn your memory verses?
NICKY:	Well, I ain't too good remembering words.
NANCY:	That's a shame! My mother says I have the best memory she's ever seen. Well, you must have done *something* right this week. How about the games? Did you do good when we played at recess?
NICKY:	No—not really. You see this Band-Aid? I fell down and got cut the first day, so I didn't get to play stuff all week.
NANCY:	Your whole week sounds like it was a waste of time to me, Nicky! You can't sing, you can't do the handcrafts, you can't memorize the Bible and you can't even play a simple game without falling on your face! What's the matter with you, Nicky? Didn't you do something right all week?
NICKY:	I accepted Jesus as my Saviour.
NANCY:	*[Silence.]* *[She starts bawling in long, loud sobs.]*
NICKY:	What's the matter, Nancy? How come girls always cry so much?
NANCY:	*[Continues sobbing, loudly.]*
NICKY:	Come on, Nancy, don't cry. Here, do you want to use my hanky?
NANCY:	Thank you. *[As she continues crying.]*
NICKY:	Why don't you blow your nose?
NANCY:	O.K. *[Blows loudly!]*
NICKY:	Now do you feel better?
NANCY:	Yes.
NICKY:	Why are you crying anyway?
NANCY:	Because that's the one thing I wanted to do this week, accept Jesus as my Saviour, but I couldn't.
NICKY:	You couldn't, why not?
NANCY:	Because I wasn't sure how.
NICKY:	It's easy to accept Jesus as your Saviour, if you really want Him. God doesn't make it hard. You already know that

	Jesus loves you very much, don't you?
NANCY:	Yes.
NICKY:	And that He died on the cross for your sins?
NANCY:	Yes, I know.
NICKY:	And it really hurt Him when He died on the cross, but He did it so you'll never have to pay for your sins. He paid it all.
NANCY:	I know it. And He wants me to be sorry for my sins.
NICKY:	Right! And if you tell Jesus you want Him, He will be your Saviour and your Friend, too. And then you'll want to do what He wants you to do.
NANCY:	I know all that, Nicky, and I want Jesus to be my Saviour and Friend. It's just that I don't know how to do it.
NICKY:	Well, I'll help you!
NANCY:	You will?
NICKY:	Sure, I'll tell you what I did. And if you really want Jesus as your Saviour you can do the same thing.
NANCY:	Tell me what you did.
NICKY:	O.K. I told Jesus that I had been bad, real bad. Then I told Him I was sorry and I wanted Him to forgive me. I told Him I was glad He died on the cross for me, but I was sorry it hurt Him. And I told Him I wanted Him to stay with me always. And you know what?
NANCY:	What?
NICKY:	He really took the bad things away, and He really stays with me. It's neat.
NANCY:	Oh, thank you, Nicky. Now I know what to do. I'm going to go talk to Jesus right now. I really thought I was something, and now I see how wrong I was. Thank you, Nicky. You're the best friend I ever had! 'Bye. *[She exits, wiping her eyes.]*
NICKY:	*[Turns toward audience and speaks in a confidential tone.]* Well, what do you know? I think I finally did something right!

NICKY AND SALLY TALK ABOUT THANKSGIVING

SCRIPTURE: Psalm 95:2
CHARACTERS: Nicky, Sally
PROPS: A silly Halloween mask for Nicky to wear

NICKY: *[Wearing mask.]* Boo! Boo! I'm scary! Boo! *[Sally comes on stage.]* My scary mask scares everyone. Hey, little boy over there. *[Nicky leans toward a boy in the audience.]* BOOOO! Oh, boy, I think I scared him. *[He turns and notices Sally.]* Oh!

SALLY: *What* are you doing?

NICKY: I'm scaring everyone with my Halloween mask!

SALLY: Don't you realize that Halloween is over! You can't make it last forever!

NICKY: Well, Halloween was fun. . . . I like to be scary.

SALLY: Well, you're a silly kid, Nicky! Look at those boys and girls in the audience. They don't still have their masks on!

NICKY: They don't? *[He looks at audience.]*

SALLY: Of course not—and neither do I—and neither does Mr. Warner. *[Substitute name of teacher.]* On Halloween he wore a funny wig, but he's certainly not wearing it now.

NICKY: Why not?

SALLY: Because Halloween is over—Dum, Dum! Boy, are you dumb! Halloween is over. See, Halloween is in October. And this is November.

NICKY: November?

SALLY: Yes, November.

NICKY: I can't wear my mask in November?

SALLY: No, you can't.

NICKY: Can I scare just one more kid before I take it off?

SALLY: Nicky, you're impossible. O.K. Just one more scare. Then you have to take it off!

NICKY: Oh, goodie. Now, let me see, who shall I scare?
[He looks out in the audience.]

SALLY:	Will you hurry up?
NICKY:	O.K. I'm ready now. *[Whispers.]* See that girl over there with the blue and white dress and the pink ribbons in her hair? *[He describes an actual girl in the audience.]*
SALLY:	*[Looks.]* Yes, I see her.
NICKY:	Well, I'm going to scare her now. Just watch and see. *[He leans toward her.]* . . . BOOOO!
SALLY:	Now, are you satisfied?
NICKY:	She didn't look very scared to me! In fact, she laughed at me.
SALLY:	Well, do you know why?
NICKY:	Why?
SALLY:	*[Loudly.]* BECAUSE HALLOWEEN IS OVER, IT IS NOVEMBER NOW, THIS IS THE MONTH WE HAVE THANKSGIVING! NO MORE HALLOWEEN. NO MORE MASKS. NO MORE TRICK OR TREAT! OVER! OVER! OVER!
	[Silence.]
NICKY:	I really have to take it off, huh?
SALLY:	That's right! Look at George over there. *[Substitute name of child in audience.]* He's looking at you. He can't believe you. *[Whispers.]* He's going to really think you are dumb if you don't get that thing off.
NICKY:	Well, O.K. *[He slowly takes mask off. Then he looks at audience.]*
SALLY:	Now, that wasn't so bad, was it?
NICKY:	No, not too bad.
SALLY:	I've got a good idea. Let's talk about Thanksgiving.
NICKY:	O.K. What shall we talk about?
SALLY:	Well, let's talk about why there is a Thanksgiving Day. Let's see if any of the kids know. Ann, do you know why we have Thanksgiving? *[She proceeds to ask various children in audience the meaning of Thanksgiving.]*
NICKY:	I know why we have Thanksgiving. The Pilgrims sailed

	across the ocean so they could worship God like they wanted to. And at first they didn't have any houses and not much food, and some of them died.
SALLY:	And then they planted crops and finally the crops grew and they were so thankful that God had given them a good crop that they decided to have a feast. And that was the first Thanksgiving in America.
NICKY:	Did they wear masks? *[Excitedly.]*
SALLY:	Of course, not, Dum, Dum.
NICKY:	Oh.
SALLY:	Anyway, Thanksgiving is a holiday every year. We have a feast and thank God for all the things He has done for us all year.
NICKY:	I have a lot of things to thank God for.
SALLY:	Me, too. What do you kids want to thank God for? *[She asks various children.]*
NICKY:	Now I'm getting all excited about Thanksgiving.
SALLY:	Well, I certainly hope so! I have to go now. Bye. *[Leaves the stage.]*
NICKY:	*[Talking confidentially to the audience.]* Listen, don't tell Sally, but I'm going to put my mask on the turkey! Bye. *[Leaves the stage.]*

BUTCH AND SALLY TALK ABOUT THE MEANING OF CHRISTMAS

SCRIPTURE: Luke 1:5-25; Luke 2:1-10

CHARACTERS: Butch, Sally
PROPS: None

SALLY: Hi, Butch.

BUTCH: Hi, Sally. We sure had fun in Sunday School today, didn't we?

SALLY: We sure did. Now that Christmas is coming soon, we're learning all about what Christmas really means. Today we learned about how a man named John was born and grew up to be the person who told everyone about Jesus.

BUTCH: Yeah, that was scary when they told about the angel talking to Zacharias. Did that *really* happen?

SALLY: Oh, yes. Every word was true!

BUTCH: How do you know?

SALLY: Because it's in the Bible.

BUTCH: Well, I'd still be scared if an angel talked to me.

SALLY: Oh, I wouldn't. Not if it was a real angel that God sent down from heaven to talk to me.

BUTCH: Well, I guess that would be all right. Hey, what are you going to get for Christmas?

SALLY: I'd like a brand new Bible of my very own—one with pictures in it of the Bible stories.

BUTCH: I want a bike and a sled and a puppy. And, lots of candy. I want so much candy it would fill my Christmas stocking all the way to the top. Don't you want more things than a Bible? Don't you want candy and nuts and toys?

SALLY: Yes, I guess so. But do you know what my favorite part of Christmas is?

BUTCH: What?

SALLY: My Mom bakes a big birthday cake with candles on it.

BUTCH: Whose birthday is it?

SALLY: It's Jesus' birthday! That's what Christmas is for, anyway— it's the time of the year we celebrate Jesus' birthday, just like when it's our birthday.

BUTCH: Do you sing too?

SALLY:	Sure we do. We sing: "Happy birthday to You; Happy birthday to You; Happy birthday dear Jesus; Happy birthday to You." And then we blow out the candles.
BUTCH:	I never thought of Christmas that way before! It's a big birthday party for Jesus. Then shouldn't we give Him presents? Instead of us wanting presents?
SALLY:	Yes. At Christmas all kids think about is what they want to get. We should be thinking of ways to please Jesus instead of ourselves.
BUTCH:	Boy, you're right, Sally. Now I feel bad for wanting so much for Christmas. What is the best, best present I could give Jesus for His birthday?
SALLY:	Do you know what Jesus wants from us more than anything at Christmas?
BUTCH:	What?
SALLY:	He wants us to love Him! And not to think of ourselves so much, but to think of others.
BUTCH:	At Christmas time I think people forget all about Jesus.
SALLY:	I know. Poor Jesus! It's His birthday and hardly anyone even thinks about Him.
BUTCH:	All they think about is presents and eating and buying stuff.
SALLY:	Poor Jesus!
BUTCH:	I'm going to go home and ask Mom to bake a birthday cake for Jesus this Christmas, so we can sing to Him.
SALLY:	And we should think about Him a lot, too, and how much we love Him.
BUTCH:	When I say my prayers, I'm going to tell Him I love Him.
SALLY:	That will be the best thing you can give Him for His birthday!
BUTCH:	This is going to be the best Christmas ever!

SALVATION AT THE SLUMBER PARTY

SCRIPTURE: Romans 10:13
CHARACTERS: Nancy, Sally
  They are dressed in nightgowns slipped over their regular clothes.
PROPS: Small comb is attached to Sally's hand with tape. It must be easy to remove during play. Cut small green construction paper dill pickle and tiny cardboard cups. Also provide a small tissue.

NANCY: I'm sure glad your Mom let you spend the night.

SALLY: Me, too.

NANCY: Let's comb each other's hair.

SALLY: O.K. I'll do yours first. Shall I make curls?

NANCY: Sure! Just like you did before.

  [Sally "combs" Nancy's hair.]

SALLY: There. Do you like that?

NANCY: Let me look in the mirror. *[Looks at herself in imaginary mirror.]* That's just perfect. Did you know that my Mom is fixing us some hot chocolate?

SALLY: Oh, good.

MOTHER'S VOICE: *[In background.]* Girls, your hot chocolate is ready.

NANCY: Thanks, Mom. We'll be right there. Let's go get it and bring it back here to my room.

SALLY: O.K.

  [Sally and Nancy exit quickly. Sally's comb is taken off her hand. Both girls get cups of hot chocolate backstage and quickly return to the stage.]

NANCY: Umm, this is good. *[Drinking hot chocolate.]* My Mom makes the best I ever tasted.

SALLY: It's delicious! Especially the baby marshmallows and whipped cream.

NANCY: You've got whipped cream on your nose!

SALLY: I do? *[Giggles.]*.

NANCY: I'll get a Kleenex.

  [Nancy leaves stage; she disposes of hot chocolate, gets a Kleenex and returns.]

NANCY:	Here, I'll get if off. *[Rubs Sally's face with Kleenex.]*
	[Sally giggles.]
NANCY:	Guess what's in the refrigerator?
SALLY:	What?
NANCY:	What's your favorite thing?
SALLY:	Not dill pickles?
NANCY:	Yes. I saved two just for us. I'll go get them.
	[Nancy quickly exits and replaces Kleenex with two dill pickles. Sally drops her mug inconspicuously while Nancy returns to stage.]
NANCY:	Here.
	[Nancy hands a pickle to Sally.]
SALLY:	Oh, thank you. This is the real sour kind that I love. *[Puts pickle to her mouth]* Ummmm, it's really good. What do you think we'll be like when we grow up?
NANCY:	I don't know. All I know is that I want to be what God wants me to be.
SALLY:	But how can you tell what that is?
NANCY:	Well, Mom and Dad say that when you want to find out what God wants you to do, you pray and ask Him to help you.
SALLY:	Then what happens?
NANCY:	Well, then He makes the things happen He wants to happen. And the things He doesn't want to happen, won't.
SALLY:	How do you know?
NANCY:	Because the Bible says that God will never let you down if you are a Christian and you love Him and you really mean it when you pray.
SALLY:	You mean if you ask Him to help you with things, He will?
NANCY:	Sure, He'll help you keep from doing wrong and He'll help you do your schoolwork.
SALLY:	And He'll even help me know what to be when I grow up?

NANCY:	Sure!
SALLY:	But, there's one problem.
NANCY:	What?
SALLY:	I don't know how to pray.
NANCY:	You don't?
SALLY:	No.
NANCY:	Haven't you ever asked Jesus to be your Saviour?
SALLY:	No.
NANCY:	Do you want to?
SALLY:	Yes.
NANCY:	Do you know that Jesus died on the cross for you, and that He was hurt so you wouldn't have to be punished?
SALLY:	Yes. That really showed He loved me, didn't it?
NANCY:	It sure did. Do you remember that verse we learned in Sunday School?
SALLY:	What verse?
NANCY:	"Whosoever shall call on the name of the Lord shall be saved." That's Romans 10:13.
SALLY:	Yes, I learned it, but what does it mean?
NANCY:	If Jesus saves you that means He takes away your sins, and makes you His child. You belong in His family. That's what "saved" means.
SALLY:	I'd like that.
NANCY:	Now you listen while I say that verse very slowly. Then you tell me what you have to do if you want Him to save you. "Whosoever shall call on the name of the Lord shall be saved." *[She says it slowly and emphatically.]*
SALLY:	I know. You have to call on the Lord.
NANCY:	That's right. Just like if you get in a mess and you call on your mother to help you.
SALLY:	I could do that. I'm in a mess because I've done wrong lots

of times. So I have to call on Jesus to help me. Is that right?

NANCY: You've got it, Sally. You've got it.

SALLY: I'm going to go kneel down by the bed and do it right now.

NANCY: Oh, Sally, I'm so happy. Then you'll belong to Jesus, too. This is the best slumber party I ever had.

[They both exit.]

BUTCH AND SALLY IN THE GRAVEYARD

SCRIPTURE: I John 3:1-3
CHARACTERS: Butch, Sally
PROPS: Large cardboard animal tooth, large cardboard animal jaw

SALLY: Hi, Butch.

BUTCH: Hi, Sally.

SALLY: Are you walking home from school?

BUTCH: Yeah, are you?

SALLY: Uh, huh. Can I walk with you?

BUTCH: Sure, only I'm going to take the shortcut home through the graveyard.

SALLY: I don't think I want to go home that way.

BUTCH: What's the matter, are you scared?

SALLY: No.

BUTCH: You are too.

SALLY:	Am not.
BUTCH:	Are too.
SALLY:	Am not.
BUTCH:	Then prove it by walking with me.
SALLY:	O.K.
BUTCH:	Come on, let's go.
SALLY:	O.K. *[Make Butch and Sally walk along.]*
BUTCH:	Well, here we are.
SALLY:	Look at all those gravestones.
BUTCH:	There's one for every person who's buried here.
SALLY:	Do you walk home this way very often?
BUTCH:	No, only on the days I'm in a hurry.
SALLY:	ACH! *[Screams.]*
BUTCH:	What's the matter with you?
SALLY:	I . . . found . . . a person's tooth!
BUTCH:	Let me see that! That's not a person's tooth, Silly, it's a horse's tooth!
SALLY:	How do you know?
BUTCH:	Did you ever see a person with a tooth THAT big? *[Holds up tooth.]*
SALLY:	No, I guess not.
BUTCH:	Now, don't be such a scaredy cat when you walk through a graveyard. You know the *real* part of a person isn't buried here anyway.
SALLY:	I know it. The real part of the person, the part that thinks and feels and knows things isn't here at all.
BUTCH:	If the person was a Christian and had Jesus in his heart, then when he died he went to Heaven to be with Jesus.
SALLY:	I know.
BUTCH:	Do you know what happens to a person who doesn't have

Jesus in his heart when he dies?

SALLY: Sure. The Bible says he will be separated from God forever and NEVER get to be with Jesus. ACH! *[Screams.]*

BUTCH: Now what?

SALLY: Look what I found this time! I think it's someone's jaw bone.

BUTCH: Sally, that's even sillier than before. Did you ever see anyone with a mouth that big?

SALLY: No, I guess not.

BUTCH: That belonged to a horse. Now, put it down and let's go home.

SALLY: O.K.

BUTCH: Sally?

SALLY: What?

BUTCH: Isn't your Grandma buried in this cemetery?

SALLY: Yes.

BUTCH: Were you sad when she died?

SALLY: Well, of course I was. Our whole family was sad. But she accepted Jesus, so now she's with Jesus.

BUTCH: It's only her body that's buried here, huh?

SALLY: Of course. The minute she died, she went right to be with Jesus. She didn't need her body anymore, and besides she's going to have a special body like the one Jesus has. It will be a perfect, healthy body with no aches or pains.

BUTCH: But, will you know her when you get to Heaven?

SALLY: Oh, sure, because the Bible says so. It's just that her body will be a much better one than she had here.

BUTCH: I'm going to be with Jesus when *I* die.

SALLY: Me, too! I'll get to see Grandma again, too. You know what, Butch?

BUTCH: What?

SALLY: I want to live the best life I can for Jesus until I die someday. I want to do all the things He wants me to do!

BUTCH: Like what?

SALLY: Well, like things that are important—like telling other people about how they can ask Jesus to be their Saviour.

BUTCH: And praying for people, and helping people and stuff like that?

SALLY: Yeah, and I want to read my Bible every day, too, cause Jesus can help us live better if we do that.

BUTCH: I read my Bible every day.

SALLY: I know you do, I do, too.

BUTCH: I can't wait to be with Jesus someday, in person, that is. I'm not afraid to die.

SALLY: Me, either!

BUTCH: Sally?

SALLY: What?

BUTCH: Are there any more chocolate chip cookies left in your cookie jar at home?

SALLY: There are if my little brother didn't beat me home.

BUTCH: But he went the long way, huh?

SALLY: Yeah.

BUTCH: Come on, let's run.

SALLY: *[Laughs.]* Butch, you're a cookie freak!

BUTCH: *[Laughs.]* I know. Let's go!

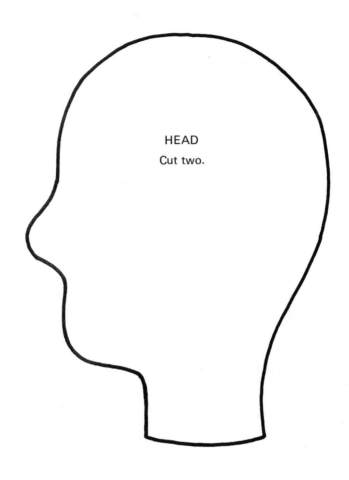

HEAD
Cut two.

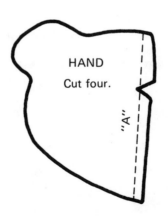

HAND
Cut four.

"A"

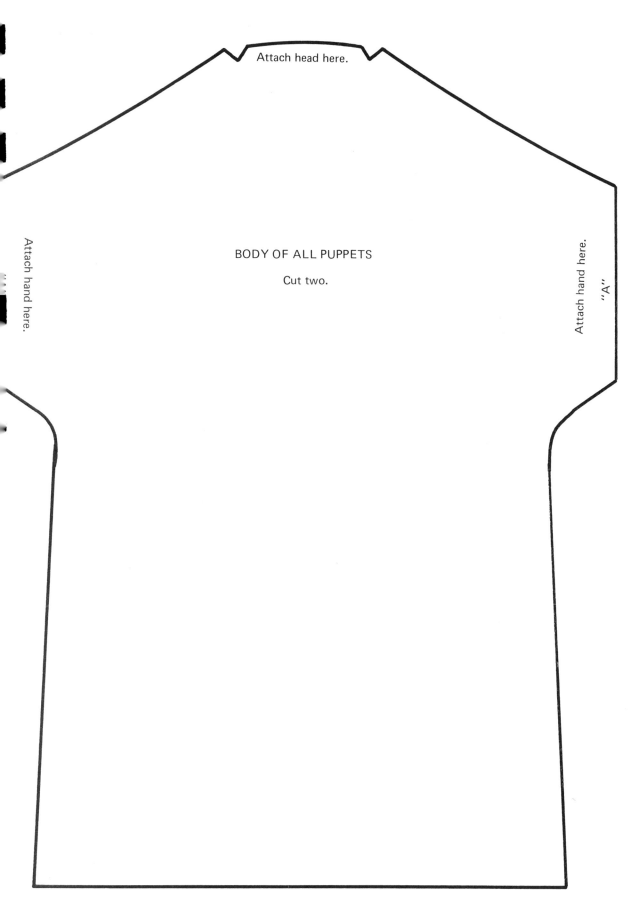

Attach head here.

BODY OF ALL PUPPETS

Cut two.

Attach hand here.

Attach hand here.

"A"

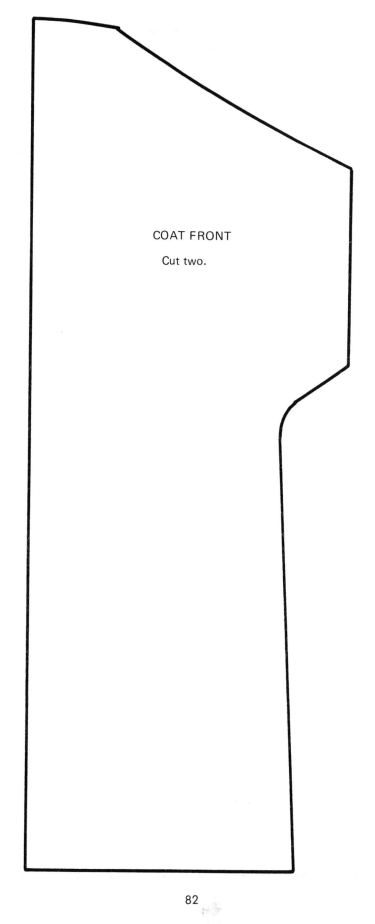

COAT FRONT

Cut two.

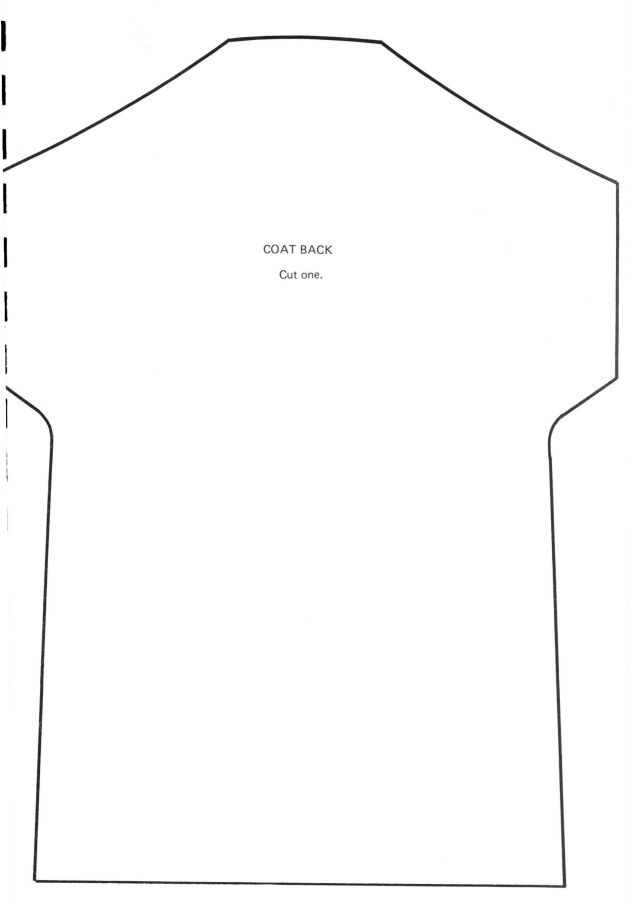

COAT BACK

Cut one.

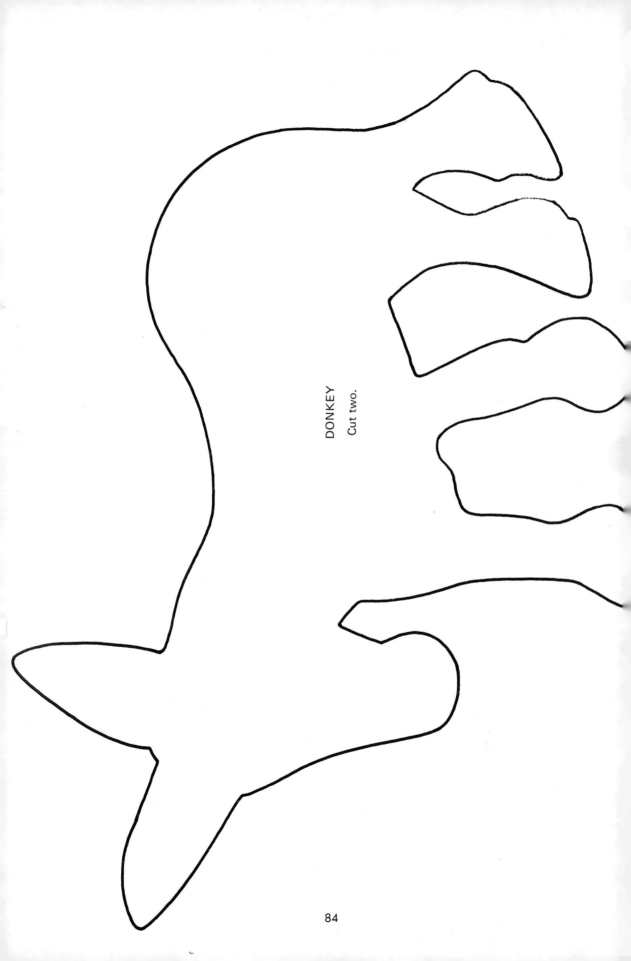

DONKEY
Cut two.